The OECD Jobs Strategy

MAKING WORK PAY
Taxation, Benefits,
Employment and Unemployment

ORGANISATION FOR ECONOMIC CO-OPERATION AND DEVELOPMENT

ORGANISATION FOR ECONOMIC CO-OPERATION AND DEVELOPMENT

Pursuant to Article 1 of the Convention signed in Paris on 14th December 1960, and which came into force on 30th September 1961, the Organisation for Economic Co-operation and Development (OECD) shall promote policies designed:

- to achieve the highest sustainable economic growth and employment and a rising standard of living in Member countries, while maintaining financial stability, and thus to contribute to the development of the world economy;
- to contribute to sound economic expansion in Member as well as non-member countries in the process of economic development; and
- to contribute to the expansion of world trade on a multilateral, non-discriminatory basis in accordance with international obligations.

The original Member countries of the OECD are Austria, Belgium, Canada, Denmark, France, Germany, Greece, Iceland, Ireland, Italy, Luxembourg, the Netherlands, Norway, Portugal, Spain, Sweden, Switzerland, Turkey, the United Kingdom and the United States. The following countries became Members subsequently through accession at the dates indicated hereafter: Japan (28th April 1964), Finland (28th January 1969), Australia (7th June 1971), New Zealand (29th May 1973), Mexico (18th May 1994), the Czech Republic (21st December 1995), Hungary (7th May 1996), Poland (22nd November 1996) and the Republic of Korea (12th December 1996). The Commission of the European Communities takes part in the work of the OECD (Article 13 of the OECD Convention).

Publié en français sous le titre :

VALORISER LE TRAVAIL

Fiscalité, prestations sociales, emploi et chômage

FOREWORD

The OECD Jobs Study concluded that unemployment was the unfortunate result of societies' failure to adapt to rapid economic change. This latest volume in the OECD Jobs Strategy series looks at how tax and benefit systems may discourage individuals to seek employment and firms to hire workers. Which groups in society face the largest disincentives to accept work offered to them, and exactly what features of tax and benefit systems cause those disincentives? A detailed examination of potential tax and benefit reforms and a survey of recent changes in OECD countries designed to improve incentives suggest a series of recommendations to policy-makers.

This report was prepared jointly by the Working Party on Tax Policy Analysis and Tax Statistics of the Committee on Fiscal Affairs and the Working Party on Social Policy of the Employment, Labour and Social Affairs Committee. It is published on the responsibility of the Secretary-General of the OECD.

TABLE OF CONTENTS

SUMMARY AND RECOMMENDATIONS

If work does not pay, people will be reluctant to work. For the majority of the population in the OECD, there are clear immediate financial incentives to work. But such incentives may be lacking for many people with low potential wages, particularly if they have children. Some will work in spite of this, because work experience improves long-run job prospects or for other reasons. Nevertheless, for these groups, social and labour market goals may clash. Benefits need to be high enough to ensure income is adequate, but this may mean that taking a job brings little or no extra income, so trapping families in a cycle of dependency.

While tax and benefit reforms cannot resolve all the fundamental causes of unemployment, tax and benefit systems can cause three types of labour-market problems. The first is the 'unemployment trap' which occurs when benefits are high compared with expected incomes when working. Cutting benefits to the unemployed would increase the reward to taking a job but the social costs of this solution may be unacceptable. The second problem is the 'poverty trap': low-wage workers have little immediate financial incentive to increase hours worked. Also, the incentive to work part-time or to invest in education and training to move up the wage ladder is blunted. The third problem is that taxes on labour may increase its cost and reduce employment. Cutting taxes on labour, even when targeted on low-wage earners, is expensive. As most reforms will have to be revenue-neutral, a switch to taxes which are not ultimately borne by wage-earners, cuts in public expenditure or a redistribution of the tax burden onto higher earners will be required.

There are no easy or obvious solutions to these problems. Reforming taxes and benefits to make work pay involves trading some policy goals against others. A mix of policies will better balance labour market, social and budgetary goals. And, of course, if jobs do not exist, people cannot find work.

No country has yet found an ideal system of taxes and benefits. Priorities vary widely across countries. This diversity offers a rich vein of experience on which countries can draw. Administrative inertia and a fear of creating losers should not inhibit experimentation. Piloting change in limited experiments allows countries to try out policy options without over-frequent, destabilising changes in tax liabilities and benefit entitlements. Such experiments -- and indeed, all policy reforms -- require careful monitoring and evaluation of outcomes.

This review of interactions between taxes, benefits, employment and unemployment leads to a series of policy recommendations. These recommendations must be tailored to the specific situations facing each Member country. Labour market problems, such as the importance of youth, long-term and seasonal unemployment, differ. Tax levels and structures vary. Reforms must respect the role played by different tiers of government. Countries have different international commitments. Nor are policies made in a vacuum. Reforms must build on current systems, targeting problem areas without unnecessarily disrupting reasonable expectations of links between social security contributions and benefits. They must be compatible with other policies designed to reduce unemployment. The eleven recommendations set out below are closely linked, particularly numbers two, three and four, which are directed at re-distributing the tax burden away from low-paid workers.

1. Out-of-work benefits should ensure that there is a reward for working

Cutting benefits is the simplest way of increasing the incentive to work, but it is not necessarily the best. If benefits are reduced to an inadequate level or if job-search is inefficiently short, poverty may increase. Nevertheless, if benefits are higher than potential in-work incomes, long-term benefit dependency out of work may be encouraged. The benefit level may need to be cut. The duration of earnings-related benefits should be designed to encourage reappraisal of acceptable wages by those who do not rapidly find work.

2. Low-wage work should not be over-taxed

In many countries, recent tax reforms have increased the tax burden on low-paid workers relative to those with high earnings. It is desirable to reverse this where possible to raise work incentives for the low-paid. Social security contributions should be restructured to reduce the burden on low earnings, or financing could be shifted to a broader tax base. But while increasing incentives to work for those without jobs, it can give those in work an incentive to reduce hours worked. The trade-off is more beneficial the wider is the earnings distribution and the lower are marginal tax rates.

3. Employment-conditional benefits should be used to increase in-work incomes of families

Such schemes are best limited to families with children because they have high replacement rates. In-work incomes of the low paid can be increased at lower budgetary cost than general tax cuts. However, as with the previous recommendation, the balance of costs and benefits depends on the structure of the labour market. Employment-conditional benefits will best be administered by whichever agency is better able to take account of particular family circumstances and deliver payments in the most cost-effective way.

4. The cost of hiring low-wage workers should be reduced

Reducing the high gap between the cost to the employer of hiring someone at a low wage rate and the return to the employee is desirable. This is particularly so in countries where the gap is relatively large or has recently been growing. Even if total labour demand is not increased, it will be shifted in favour of the low-wage, hard-to-employ group. (See, however, the caveats under the previous two recommendations.) Other labour market policies might usefully be co-ordinated with this change.

5. Job search should be policed effectively

Efficient policing of job-search requirements is essential whatever the benefit level. Integrating administration of job-search requirements with active labour market policies can enhance the efficacy of both (for details, see the review of 'Enhancing the Effectiveness of Active Labour Market Policies').

6.   Non-employment benefits should not be used as alternative unemployment benefits

The use of benefits which do not require active job search -- such as sickness-related and early retirement benefits -- as alternatives to unemployment benefits should be restricted. Subsidised early retirement should not be used to encourage workers out of the labour force.

7.   Transitions between unemployment and work should be facilitated

Even when incomes in work are higher than out of work, people may fear greater insecurity if they take a job. Slow processing of claims for benefits in work and abrupt withdrawal of non-cash benefits paid to those without jobs can create additional hurdles for those attempting to enter employment. Penalising those newly employed by withholding disproportionate amounts of tax at source has a similar effect.

8.   The relationship between incomes in work and out of work should be made clearer

If other recommendations are followed, individuals will be better off in employment than out of work receiving benefit. But if systems remain as complex as they are at present, individuals are unlikely to know by how much. Simpler rules, better co-ordination between tax and benefit systems and co-operation between different agencies combined with publicity campaigns, will illustrate that work is financially rewarding.

9.   Part-time work should be encouraged for targeted groups through the benefit system

Part-time work which promotes contact with the labour market should be encouraged for those such as lone-parents or the long-term unemployed for whom full-time work may not be a realistic option. Increasing earnings disregards (the amount of earnings ignored in means-tests) and allowing part-time work to be combined with reduced benefit receipt for a limited period will help such groups. But experience suggests that it is important to maintain tight controls on part-time unemployment benefits to guard against abuses.

10.   Spouses of the unemployed should have an incentive to work

Insurance benefits are usually based on the income of the individual, means-tested benefits on that of the family. The number of recipients of means-tested benefits has increased rapidly in nearly every OECD country because of failure to qualify for and exhaustion of insurance benefits, growth in youth unemployment and in the number of lone-parent families. Depending on the design of means-tests, it can reduce the incentive to work part-time or for low earnings not just by the unemployed person but also by their spouse. Means-tested benefits should be designed so that each member of the household has an incentive to work, for example, by separating benefit entitlements for individuals.

## 11.	The financing of benefits should be transparent

The link between the level and structure of benefits and how they are financed is too obscure to be comprehensible to many people. This is particularly so in countries where social benefits are financed mainly by levies on employers. Various policies can inform the debate on reforming benefit systems by making the costs of benefits clearer. Details of the social contributions paid by employers could be itemised on pay-slips. More substantial reforms, such as switching contributions from employers to employees, or risk-rating employers' contributions, could also be considered.

Chapter 1

INTRODUCTION

Taxes and benefits are the most direct way for governments to affect the financial incentives for individuals to work and for employers to hire them. But existing tax and benefit systems owe many of their features to a bygone era and have failed to keep pace with changes in the labour market.

The OECD *Jobs Study* highlighted tax and benefit systems as an important cause of present problems of the labour market. Taxes increase the costs of employing workers, particularly low-wage workers; benefit systems are alleged to leave little incentive to work, especially for low-wage families. Tax and benefit systems may fail to 'make work pay'.

1. This Thematic Review highlights three ways in which taxes and benefits can cause labour market disincentives.

   – *Unemployment trap*: benefits paid to the unemployed and their families are high relative to potential earnings so they have little incentive to find a job.

   – *Poverty trap:* incremental increases in earnings or income lead to withdrawal of benefits and higher tax payments, so people on low incomes receiving benefits are discouraged from additional effort.

   – *High labour costs:* tax payments and social security contributions for those on low earnings are high, raising the cost of labour and discouraging hiring.

The existing features of tax and benefit systems that cause these disincentives in Member countries are considered in turn and then possible reforms are reviewed. But tax and benefit systems can only be restructured to reduce the damage they do to the labour market when this is consistent with their fundamental purpose. Taxes must raise revenues and benefits are mostly intended to provide for those with insufficient incomes. Nearly all reforms which 'make work pay' involve trade-offs between these fundamental objectives. Reforms of the tax and benefit system require political judgements, not just positive analysis.

The report approaches immediate financial incentives to work as a key determinant of labour market behaviour. Clearly, other factors also influence whether people work or not. Sometimes rational people will work even where this seems, at first sight, to be irrational. Even if there is no immediate financial reward to working, a low-paid job might nevertheless be the first step on the ladder towards higher earnings. People might also wish to work because they *like* working. Also, paid employment structures one's social life to an important degree, through valuable networks, and gives meaning to personal existence. Furthermore, many of the financial incentives discussed in this report refer to workers and the unemployed, rather than employers. Many unemployed in the

OECD might find this a topsy-turvy way of viewing their problem; they are actively looking for work, but jobs are not available for them at any wage.

However, incentives are important as well, for three reasons. The first is that financial incentives matter *at the margin*. Of course people take a long-term view of their employment prospects, and obviously many like their jobs, but financial incentives still matter. Many people will look for work even if they would get more money receiving benefits, but even more will seek work were there is a clear financial incentive to do so. After all, if work does not pay, individuals exchange leisure for a financial set-back. The implied negative value of free time goes against common experience. Secondly, taking up work involves costs for travel, work, clothing and equipment and possibly child care. If work does not pay, those with very few resources may not be able to afford to undertake it without denying resources to their children. Partly for this reason, employers will not offer jobs at wages which they know that no-one could accept without being worse off than they would be were they to remain unemployed. The third argument for discussing financial incentives to work is that empirical studies show that incentives matter. The report will refer to some of these studies.

It is not argued that taxes and benefits are the cause of all unemployment and that appropriate reforms will return OECD countries to full-employment. How could this be the case, when some countries have followed some of the prescriptions suggested, but unemployment has nevertheless risen or remained stubbornly high? The *Jobs Study* showed that the malaise in the labour market stems from many causes.

Medium and long-term impacts of tax and benefit reforms are considered -- policies that affect equilibrium or core unemployment, not short-term, cyclical movements around the core level. In the short term, increased labour market participation of the 'non-employed' may increase unemployment. But output in the medium-term is determined by the volume of labour as well as its productivity, so increasing labour supply is desirable.

Finally, benefit administration and the links between the benefit system and active labour market policies are not discussed in this report. For a detailed review of recent experience, see OECD, 1996*c*.

Chapter 2

TAXES, BENEFITS AND CHANGES IN THE LABOUR MARKET

An official Australian paper recently stated, in proposing major reforms,

Social Security arrangements for unemployed people still largely reflect the unemployment benefit system introduced in the 1940s, around the time of the release of the White Paper on Full Employment [in 1945]. (Australia, 1994, p. 143).

This observation applies with equal justification to most OECD Member countries. Unemployment benefits were designed for situations where unemployment was infrequent and of limited duration, and youth unemployment and lone-parent families (other than widows) were not of policy concern. Other areas of social policy -- housing, early retirement, and invalidity -- could be treated as separate from the support given to the unemployed. The welfare system was designed for a population where participation rates were high among men and low among women, and people could expect an uninterrupted working life. Cyclical variation in employment was to a substantial degree absorbed by women withdrawing from the labour market during recessions.

In these circumstances, it was relatively easy to design benefit systems to be welfare-enhancing. Risk averse individuals wanted insurance against loss of earnings and were content to pay premiums related to expected calls on the benefit system. Benefits were only needed for some limited amount of time; new work would be found relatively quickly.

There have been some major changes to OECD labour markets since benefit systems were designed. Benefit systems have responded to these changes by distinguishing between a greater variety in labour market and family situations and differentiating according to labour market and family situation. But the causation does not flow in one direction: wages and employment also respond to the structure of the tax and benefit system. The most important changes in labour markets are:

- Unemployment is generally at a much higher level than when current unemployment insurance schemes were put in place after 1945. Averaging around ten million (3 per cent of the labour force) in the OECD area between 1950 and 1975, it is now nearly 35 million, or 8 per cent of the labour force (OECD, 1994*b*).

- One-third of the unemployed has been out of work for more than a year in around half of OECD countries. Many who lose jobs suffer extended bouts of unemployment and exhaust their basic unemployment benefit entitlement (OECD, 1995*d*).

- The average increase in the youth (under 25) unemployment rate between 1973-1975 and 1993-1994 was 13 percentage points (OECD, 1995*d*). Youths currently constitute around one-third of all the unemployed. They have limited or no work experience: they have not contributed to insurance schemes and so are often not entitled to these benefits.

– Since 1966, labour force participation of men has declined in all OECD regions, from over 90 per cent of men aged 25 to 64 to around 80 per cent in 1994 (OECD, 1994*b* and OECD 1995*e*). Many of those withdrawing from the labour force nevertheless receive benefits for invalidity, sickness or early retirement. Female participation over the same period has grown in most OECD regions, from 40 to 60 per cent, with massive increases in most of those countries where female participation was relatively low.

– As a result, two-earner couples are more common. In the United States, two-earner households have increased from 9 to 40 per cent of the total since 1940 (Hayghe, 1990). Since 1983, the proportion of two-adult households where both adults work has increased from 40 to 49 per cent in 12 OECD countries (Belgium, Canada, France, Germany, Greece, Ireland, Italy, Luxembourg, Netherlands Portugal, Spain and the United Kingdom). The number of households where one adult works and one does not fell from 51 to 42 percent (Gregg and Wadsworth, 1996).

– Lone-parent families have become more common. Their numbers have doubled in almost all OECD countries since the early 1970s (more than doubled in Germany, Ireland, the United Kingdom and the United States) and accounted for 15 per cent of all families with children in 1990-1991 (OECD, 1993*b*, Ermisch, 1990, Eurostat, 1995).

– Together, the increasing numbers of two-earner couples and lone-parent families have meant that the traditional model of the working man supporting wife and children has become ever less typical, declining from 70 per cent to 20 per cent of households in the United States since 1940 (Hayghe, 1990). Insuring individual workers against loss of wages is less effective in ensuring adequate family incomes and well-being when increasing numbers of households of working age are not part of the labour force.

– Part-time work has grown, accounting for a fifth of all employment in a third of OECD countries (OECD, 1995*d*). The relationship of the benefit system to part-time work is complex. Not all part-time workers are entitled to insurance benefits, leaving a gap in the coverage of the working population by the insurance benefit system. Sometimes working part-time is consistent with benefit receipt, sometimes it is not.

– The earnings distribution narrowed in the 1960s and 1970s in most OECD countries. In the 1980s it appears to have widened markedly in a number of countries, particularly the United Kingdom, the United States, Canada, Australia, New Zealand and Japan (OECD 1993*a*). Since 1990 there has been an unambiguous increase in earnings inequality only in the United Kingdom (OECD 1996*a*). In Canada and the United States, real wages at the bottom of the distribution have fallen, whereas elsewhere they have remained static or continued to increase. There has been little or no change in the earnings distribution in the Nordic countries, France and Germany. Without benefit income, some families with a single full-time earner might not reach a socially acceptable standard of living. The dispersion of the distribution of original income (*i.e.* before taxes and transfer payments) has widened since 1980 in Australia, Japan, the Netherlands, Sweden, the United Kingdom and the United States (see OECD, 1995*g*).

14

However, in some countries the tax and benefit system has ensured that changes in the distribution of disposable incomes of households have after all been relatively small.

As working and family patterns have become more diverse, so have the types of benefits received. Figure 1 shows that although unemployment benefits are the largest single form of social expenditure directed at people below retirement age, they account for little more than 20 per cent on average across the OECD. Family benefits, other income maintenance programmes and disability benefits are all often individually more important than is unemployment benefit.

Figure 1: Distribution of Social Outlays
Expenditures as a percentage of Outlays directed towards the non-aged population (1993)

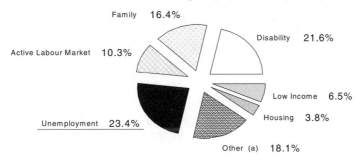

a) Other: Sickness, Maternity, and Occupational Injury & Disease.
Source: OECD Social Expenditure Data Base.

Tax systems have also undergone major changes. Governments' revenue needs have increased dramatically: from an average of 26 per cent in OECD countries in 1965, to 35 per cent in 1980 and to 39 per cent now (OECD, 1996*b*). Tax structures have also changed. Table 1 shows a reduction in the role of property taxes and corporate income tax. General consumption taxes, like VAT, have tended to substitute for other taxes on goods and services, such as excises and duties. Despite different economic, social and fiscal policies, these patterns are found in nearly all OECD countries. But it is the share of social security contributions in the tax mix that shows the largest increase, to 27 per cent of total revenues in 1993. Taxes on personal incomes increased from an average of 7.1 to 11.3 per cent of GDP in the OECD between 1965 and 1993, and social security contributions swelled from 4.9 to 10.2 per cent of GDP. The personal income tax has tended to move from taxing families to taxing individuals and tax thresholds have often fallen relative to earnings, bringing more employees into the tax net. Ceilings on social security contributions have been raised or eliminated. These developments have changed the way the tax system interacts with benefits and the way in which tax and benefit systems affect work decisions (see OECD, 1995*a*).

The debate about the links between the tax and benefit system and the labour market is often reduced to a discussion of whether unemployment benefits are high compared with earnings and whether they imply significant work disincentives. These issues, important as they are, fail to do justice to the full complexity of the real world. Disposable incomes in and out of work depend on social security contributions, taxes paid on earnings and benefits, and entitlement to other often means-tested benefits (housing, child-care, lone parents, *etc.*). As succeeding sections will show, such an over-simplification can move the discussion away from other important effects of the tax and benefit system on the labour market. Reforms to make work pay do not necessarily involve such sharp trade-offs between social and labour market objectives.

Table 1. **Structure of taxation in OECD countries, 1965-1995**

Per cent of total revenue	1965	1970	1975	1980	1985	1990	1995
Personal income	26	28	30	31	30	29	27
Corporate income	9	9	8	8	8	8	8
Social security	18	20	22	22	22	23	25
Property	8	7	6	5	5	6	5
General consumption	12	14	13	14	16	17	18
Other goods and services	26	22	19	18	18	14	15

Notes: OECD average of the percentage of taxation from each source. Payroll taxes (3 000) are included with social security contributions (2 000). Excludes taxes under the residual (6 000) category. Figures do not therefore add to 100.
Source: OECD (1997).

Chapter 3

THE UNEMPLOYMENT TRAP

3.1   Replacement rates

The unemployment benefit system provides insurance against job loss which individuals would find difficult, if not impossible, to negotiate with private insurers. This is a source of welfare gains. Benefits also allow the unemployed to search for a job which matches their abilities, rather than being forced by financial hardship into accepting the first available job offer. Having the right people in the right jobs raises productivity and reduces the chance of them becoming unemployed in the future. In this way, unemployment benefits can help labour markets work effectively.

But unemployment benefits can also have negative effects on labour markets and social welfare. By freeing the unemployed from having to take less ideal jobs, they increase the duration of unemployment. Unemployment benefits also alter incentives in wage bargaining. If the financial consequences of unemployment are harsh, workers will be wary of pushing up wages and so risking their jobs. Unemployment benefits also subsidise seasonal employment patterns. Without countervailing factors (such as appropriate policy measures), the higher benefits are relative to earnings (the so-called 'replacement rate'), the higher unemployment will be.[1]

3.1.1   *Have unemployment benefit systems become more generous?*

As part of the *Jobs Study*, an index was constructed for almost all OECD Member countries, summarising gross (*i.e.*, before-tax) unemployment benefit entitlements relative to (gross) earnings. This index averages across gross replacement rates for two different earnings levels, three family types and three durations of unemployment. It was found that growth in unemployment benefit entitlements, from an OECD average of 16 per cent of earnings in 1961 to 29 per cent in 1991, could have contributed to the rise in unemployment. But if there is a causal connection, there is a time lag of many years before the full effects are felt. The OECD *Jobs Study* concluded, "this comparison (between unemployment benefits and aggregate unemployment rates) suggests that although there is not an immediate statistical link between unemployment rates and unemployment benefit entitlements, the hypothesis of a longer-term link is plausible." (OECD, 1994*b*). However, using the same data, Blondal and Pearson (1995) find that higher benefits are statistically associated with higher labour force participation and that there is no statistically significant effect of the index on the employment-to-population ratio.

Figure 2 updates this series to 1995. The index does not indicate that the response of most governments to high and persistent unemployment has been to cut benefit entitlements (see Box 1). Indeed, the area-wide summary index has risen slightly, to 31 per cent in 1995.

17

Figure 2. Index of benefit entitlements, 1961-1995[1][2]
Percentages

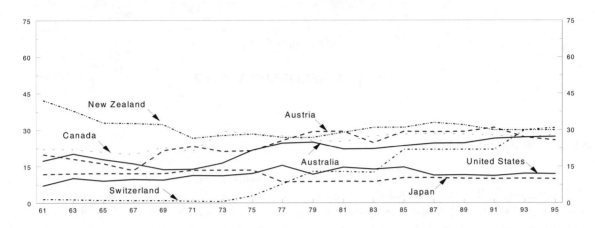

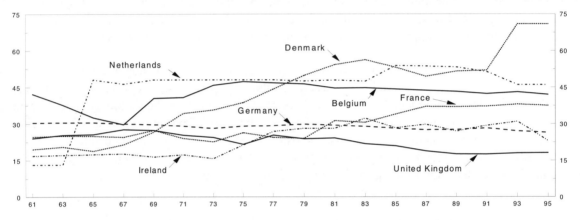

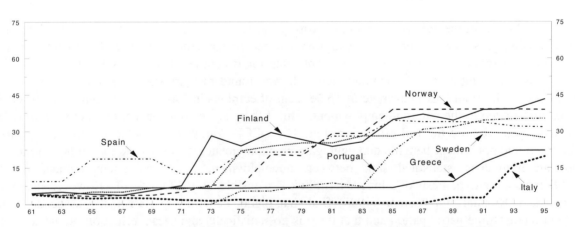

1. The average of the unemployment benefit replacement rates for two earnings levels, three family situations and three durations of unemployment. For further details, see OECD, *The OECD Jobs Study: Evidence and Explanations, Chapter 8.* The earnings data used to compute replacement rates for 1995 are Secretariat estimates.

2. Final year data refer to 1994 for the United States.

Source: OECD Database on Unemployment Benefit Entitlements and Replacement Rates.

Box 1. Recent changes in unemployment benefit systems and their impact on the index of benefit entitlements

The index is an average of replacement rates, calculated at average earnings and two-thirds of average earnings, for people unemployed for one year, for two to three years and for four to five years, and for single people, married people with an employed spouse, and married people with an unemployed spouse. The index does not give an average level of *actual* unemployment benefit receipts. For example, a cut in entitlement in the fourth and fifth year of unemployment would affect very few of the actual unemployed, but would have a relatively large effect on the index. The index is, on the other hand, a good indicator of the generosity of a country's unemployment benefit system. If high benefits were paid in the first months of unemployment but nothing thereafter, most people, actual and potential recipients, would conclude that it is a less generous system than one which paid a lower level of benefit indefinitely. However, average benefit receipt would be higher in the former system than in the latter. It is perfectly possible for changes in the benefit system to have resulted in budgetary savings while at the same time increasing the index of unemployment benefit entitlements. (For more discussion, see Chapter 8 of the OECD Jobs Study.)

Some recent changes in benefit systems and their effects on the index are as follows:

Australia: A shift to independent entitlements for husband and wife and reduction in benefit withdrawal rates in 1995. Both changes make it easier for a member of the household to have some earnings without losing all benefit entitlements. Earnings are assumed to be high in the 'working spouse' case in the index, so the changes have had no effect on the measure.

Austria: Reduction in maximum benefit levels in 1993. Minimum contribution period increased to 26 weeks in 1995.

Belgium: Recent restrictions in access to benefits and tighter policing of job search are not captured by the index.

Canada: A reduction in benefit amounts for couples in 1993.

Denmark: Extensions in the legal duration of benefit entitlements to seven years in 1994 have increased the index markedly. However, it was relatively easy in the 1980s to re-qualify for the benefit through public work and training programmes. The de jure change has been to increase the generosity of the scheme whereas the de facto effect may have been to reduce it.

Finland: Means-testing of the basic unemployment allowance was ended in 1994. The Labour Market Support benefit introduced in 1994 has increased gross benefit entitlement.

France: The level of benefit declines the longer someone is unemployed. Benefit reductions are now smaller but more frequent than previously. The system is more generous in the second year of unemployment, less generous in years four and five of unemployment than previously. But the net effect has been to raise the index slightly.

Germany: The insurance benefit was reduced in 1993 by three percentage points for single people and one percentage point for couples.

Greece: Eligibility conditions changed making it easier to get longer UI benefits in 1989 and UA benefit entitlement was extended in 1991, increasing the index,

Ireland: Benefits were increased more rapidly than inflation until 1993; in 1995 the earnings-related element was abolished.

Italy: In 1991, a mobility benefit was introduced for certain categories of the unemployed. Mobility benefit is included in the OECD index, unlike the benefit for short-time working, the Cassa Integrazione Guadagni Straordinaria, which is not included because its recipients were not formally counted as unemployed. The basic unemployment benefit was increased in stages to 30 per cent and then to 40 per cent of average earnings over the previous three years. An average of mobility and ordinary benefit based on the number of recipients has been used in the index.

Netherlands: Conditions for receipt of earnings-related insurance benefits were tightened in 1993. The work test in social assistance was tightened in 1996.

New Zealand: In 1991, benefits were reduced (for example, by 25 per cent for young single adults). Tests and sanctions were tightened and waiting periods increased.

Portugal: Increased entitlement.

Spain: A reform in 1993 altered contribution periods and rate structures. The index decreased.

Switzerland: Duration increased in 1993 with a small cut in the replacement rate. The overall effect of the changes has been to increase the index.

The index does not capture all changes in unemployment benefit generosity (its limitations are discussed in detail in OECD 1994*b*). In particular, it focuses on changes in benefit levels and durations, not on eligibility or administrative controls on job-search requirements. For example, since 1979, Belgium, Denmark, France, Germany, Greece, the Netherlands, Sweden, Switzerland and the United Kingdom have all increased the period of employment required to qualify for unemployment insurance. In Belgium benefit can now be suspended if the recipient has been in receipt of benefit for more than one-and-a-half times the regional average duration by sex and age.

Table 2 summarises the situation in 1995 for 18 countries[2], giving initial gross replacement rates for a single person and a married couple with no children with average earnings in work. The lowest replacement rates are found in Australia, Ireland, Italy, New Zealand and the United Kingdom. (The overall index presented in Figure 2 gives rather lower figures, reflecting the exhaustion or reduction of benefits in longer durations of unemployment.)

Table 2 does not take account of taxation, benefits to children, social assistance, employment-conditional transfers or housing benefits. Together these have a large impact on the ratio of incomes in an out of work, as succeeding sections will show.

Table 2. **Gross replacement rates, 1994/1995**

Per cent	Single	Couple
Australia	24	43
Belgium	38	38
Canada	55	55
Denmark	60	60
Finland	52	52
France	58	58
Germany	37	42
Ireland	24	38
Italy	30	30
Japan	52	52
Netherlands	70	70
New Zealand	22	37
Norway	62	62
Spain	70	70
Sweden	77	77
Switzerland	70	70
United Kingdom	16	26
United States	50	50

Note: Replacement rates refer to the main unemployment benefits. Where social assistance benefits are higher than unemployment benefits, it is assumed that the family receives unemployment benefits, *i.e.,* their assets disqualify them because of social assistance means tests. The worker is assumed to be 40 years old and to have worked continuously since age 18. Replacement rates are for the first month of unemployment after waiting periods have been met.
Source: OECD Database on Taxation and Benefit Entitlements.

3.1.2 Taxation and typical net replacement rates

When full taxes and social security contributions are levied on benefits out of work, progressive tax-rate schedules mean that the average tax rate in work is higher than out of work. In some countries, the differential effect is larger because social security contributions and income taxes are not levied on benefits, or they are levied at a reduced rate. Table 3 shows the tax treatment of unemployment insurance and assistance benefits in 25 countries. Three countries -- the Czech Republic, Japan and Portugal -- do not levy income taxes on benefits. Belgium and Greece offer tax concessions on benefit income relative to earned income, in addition to the automatic effect from tax schedules. In Austria and Germany, unemployment benefits are set as a proportion of previous after-tax earnings. Benefits are subject to tax in Australia, Ireland and the United Kingdom, but the level of the benefits is below tax thresholds. Many more countries exempt benefit income from social security contributions. Only in Canada, Finland, Greece, Hungary, the Netherlands, Sweden and Switzerland are full contributions levied, although a further eight countries charge reduced contributions.

Table 3. Tax treatment of benefits

	Unemployment insurance	Unemployment assistance
Australia	none	T(n)S(n)[1]
Austria	*	*
Belgium	T(reduced)	none
Canada	TS	none
Czech Republic	-	none
Denmark	TS(reduced)	none
Finland	TS	TS
France	TS(reduced)	T(n)S(n)
Germany	*	*
Greece	T(reduced)S	T(reduced)S
Hungary	TS	none
Iceland	TS(reduced)	none
Ireland	T	-
Italy	T	none
Japan	-	none
Luxembourg	TS(reduced)	none
Netherlands	TS	TS
New Zealand	none	T
Norway	TS(reduced)	none
Portugal	-	-
Spain	TS(reduced)	T(n)
Sweden	TS	TS
Switzerland	TS	none
United Kingdom	T(n)	none
United States	T	none

Notes: 'T' indicates taxable, 'S' that social security contributions are payable; '-' that neither tax nor social security contributions are levied; 'T(n)' that the system is structured so that a long-term recipient will not pay because credits, allowances or zero-rate bands exceed the benefit level; '(reduced)' indicates that a reduced rate is payable for beneficiaries; 'none' indicates that there is no specific scheme; and '*' that unemployment insurance and assistance are set as a proportion of after-tax income.

1.   *The social security contribution referred to is the Medicare levy.*

Source: OECD Database on Taxation and Benefit Entitlements.

Table 4. **Average rate of income tax and social security contributions on incomes in and out of work, 1994**

Per cent of gross income	Family type	Average tax rate	
		benefits	earnings
Australia	Single	0	23
	Couple	0	22
Austria	Single	0	26
	Couple	0	20
Canada	Single	21	27
	Couple	13	17
Denmark	Single	37	45
	Couple	27	37
Finland	Single	25	38
	Couple	27	38
France	Single	9	28
	Couple	6	21
Germany	Single	0	40
	Couple	0	29
Ireland	Single	0	29
	Couple	0	22
Japan	Single	0	14
	Couple	0	11
Luxembourg	Single	22	25
	Couple	8	12
Netherlands	Single	37	40
	Couple	32	37
New Zealand	Single	15	24
	Couple	15	22
Norway	Single	25	30
	Couple	16	25
Portugal	Single	0	18
	Couple	0	14
Sweden	Single	34	33
	Couple	34	33
Switzerland	Single	15	23
	Couple	9	17
United Kingdom	Single	0	27
	Couple	0	25
United States	Single	14	26
	Couple	4	19

Notes and source: see Table 2.

Table 4 indicates the effect of these different treatments in practice and the impact of credits and allowances and progressive rate schedules on incomes in and out of work. The Table shows the taxes and social security contributions paid by someone with average earnings. The average tax rate is also calculated for the benefits that this person would receive were they to become unemployed. In nearly every case (the exception being Sweden), the average tax rate on benefit income is lower than on earnings. In Australia, Austria, Germany, Ireland and Portugal, and for single people in Japan and the United Kingdom, average tax rates on benefits are zero. In some cases -- for example, Austria and Germany -- this is due to tax exemption of benefits, whereas in others -- Australia and Ireland --

this arises because benefits are below the starting threshold for paying tax. Only in Sweden are average taxes paid on benefits similar to those paid when in work (the apparently anomolous higher tax rates on benefits being explained by a tax allowance to cover work expenses).

Table 5 shows the impact of taxes and social security contributions on work incentives measured by replacement rates. For a single person and married couple, the Table gives replacement rates before and after the tax-and-contribution effect. On average, replacement rates net of tax are around eight percentage points higher than measured before tax. Only in Sweden and the Netherlands net replacement rates are below gross rates.

This pattern varies between countries due both to the level and structure of taxes and social security contributions. In those where both benefits and earnings are subject to full taxes and social security contributions, net replacement rates are only slightly lower than gross replacement rates (the average difference in replacement rates being around four percentage points). In the countries where benefits are taxed but either reduced or no social security contributions are payable, net replacement rates are significantly higher than are gross rates. The largest differences are found in Germany and Japan (because neither tax nor social security contributions are payable), Belgium and France (where social security contributions are relatively high and the concessions given to those on benefits significantly reduce the amount of contributions payable).

Table 5. **Replacement rates before and after tax by family type, 1994**

Replacement rate (%)	Single person		Couple no children	
	Gross	Net	Gross	Net
Australia	24	30	43	50
Belgium	38	65	38	57
Canada	55	58	55	64
Denmark	60	70	60	70
Finland	52	63	52	63
France	58	67	58	70
Germany	37	68	42	61
Ireland	24	34	38	49
Italy	30	36	30	42
Japan	52	63	52	61
Netherlands	70	69	70	69
New Zealand	22	25	37	41
Norway	62	66	62	67
Spain	70	72	70	73
Sweden	77	75	77	75
Switzerland	70	73	70	73
United Kingdom	16	23	26	36
United States	50	58	50	60

Notes: Gross rates are identical to those reported in Table 2. The net replacement rate for a single person in the Netherlands is lower than the gross replacement rate due to the 'compensation allowance', a supplement to gross wages paid by employers to compensate for a switch from employer to employee social security contributions. Also see Table 2 for other notes. In Germany, UI is calculated on the basis of individual tabulated net income. The lower net replacement rate for a couple reflects the favourable tax treatment for joint-filing by couples in work. The net replacement rates are lower than gross replacement rates in Sweden because of the earned income tax allowance.
Source: OECD Database on Taxation and Benefit Entitlements.

3.1.3   *Typical net replacement rates for different family types*

Table 6 shows the structure of support for dependent spouses and children provided through tax and benefits systems. Nearly all countries offer some kind of cash transfer contingent on having children. These transfers are sometimes universal and so paid to all families with children, in other cases they are means-tested and so withdrawn from those on higher incomes, and sometimes transfers combine universal and means-tested elements. Few unemployment insurance systems offer supplements for a dependent spouse (five out of 22), although around half adjust benefits to take account of dependent children. These supplements are rather more common in unemployment assistance schemes, with six out of 12 taking account of a dependent spouse and eight of dependent children. Finally, most countries take account of family status in the tax system. Of the 25 shown, 19 have either an allowance, a credit or a separate rate schedule for married couples, and 16 offer some kind of concession to families with children.

Table 6. **Support for families with children through the tax and benefit system**

	Child Benefits	Unemployment Insurance		Unemployment Assistance		Tax (Allowance/Credit/Other)	
		supplement for spouse	for children	supplement for spouse	for children	for spouse	for children
Australia	income-tested	none		yes	yes	C	-
Austria	universal	yes	yes	yes	yes	C	C
Belgium	universal	yes[1]	yes[1]	none		C	C
Canada	-	-	-	none		C	C
Czech Republic	universal/income-tested	-	-	none		A	A
Denmark	universal	-	-	none		-	-
Finland	universal	-	yes	-	yes	-	-
France	universal	-	-	no	no	O	O
Germany	income-tested	-	yes	-	yes	O	A
Greece	in-work	yes	yes	yes	yes	-	-
Hungary	universal	-	-	none		-	A
Iceland	universal/income-tested	-	yes	none		C	-
Ireland	universal	yes	yes	yes	yes	AO	A
Italy	income-tested	-	-	none		C	C
Japan	income-tested	-	-	none		A	A
Luxembourg	universal	-	yes	none		O	O
Netherlands	universal	-	-	-	-	A	-
New Zealand	income-tested	none		yes	yes	-	-
Norway	universal	-	yes	none		O	C
Portugal	universal	-	-	yes	yes	AC	AC
Spain	income-related	+	+	-	-	C	C
Sweden	universal	-	-	-	-	-	-
Switzerland	labour force	no	no	none		AO	A
United Kingdom	universal	yes	-	none		C	-
United States	income-tested	-	-	none		A	-

Notes: In-work means the benefit is by employers, labour force that the benefit is paid by employers or the unemployment insurance fund. None indicates no specific scheme, - that there is no specific element in a scheme. C indicates a tax credit, A an allowance and O some other form of support (*e.g.,* a different tax schedule is applied). A + indicates that the minimum varies between different family types.
1.   Dependents supplement, with different minima and maxima.
Source: OECD Database on Taxation and Benefit Entitlements.

Different types of support will have different effects on work incentives. Universal child benefits will only have a small effect as they are paid regardless of employment status. Incomes in and out of work rise by the same amount and so replacement rates are marginally higher. Means-tested benefits provide a work disincentive. Earned income leads to reductions in means-tested benefits, depending on the structure of the income test. Supplements to unemployment insurance and assistance benefits increase income out of work and so provide a work disincentive. Tax credits and allowances are more likely to have the opposite effect, raising income in work more than out of work income. To obtain maximum benefit from an allowance or a wasteable tax credit, incomes need to exceed the value of the credit or allowance. In many cases, benefit income would be below this threshold and so those out of work do not gain while those in work gain in full.

Table 7. **Work incentives for different family types and the effect of support for families with children**

Replacement rate (%)	Couple no children	Couple 2 children
Australia	50	64
Belgium	57	61
Canada	64	66
Denmark	70	73
Finland	63	75
France	70	73
Germany	61	71
Ireland	49	65
Italy	42	47
Japan	61	59
Netherlands	69	71
New Zealand	41	57
Norway	67	73
Spain	73	75
Sweden	75	78
Switzerland	73	84
United Kingdom	36	41
United States	60	60

Notes and source: see Table 2.

Table 7 indicates the effect of support for families with children on replacement rates. In nearly every case, the replacement rate for families with children is higher than without, by an average of eight percentage points. Very small or no differences occur in Belgium, Canada, Denmark, France, Japan, the Netherlands, Spain, Sweden and the United States. The reason for this varies. In Belgium, France, the Netherlands and Sweden, child benefits are paid universally. Belgium, France Japan and Spain offer child-related tax concessions which, as noted above, are likely to raise incomes in work proportionally more than out of work. In the United States, there are no child benefits for families with work, nor for unemployment insurance recipients. In Australia, Ireland, New Zealand and the United Kingdom, replacement rates are substantially (around 15 percentage points) higher for families with children. This reflects the absence of child-related tax concessions in all countries from this group, but Ireland (where the effect is offset by child supplements to unemployment insurance). In Australia and New Zealand, child benefits are means-tested. In the absence of employment income, incomes of families with children are therefore higher than are incomes for families without children. Where there is employment, the value of the child benefit is reduced, so the difference in incomes of families with or without children is reduced. Thus, replacement rates are relatively high for families with children.

3.1.4   *Housing support and typical net replacement rates*

Housing-related assistance can add significantly to out of work (and sometimes to in-work) income. Table 8 shows the systems of housing-related cash transfers operated in different countries. Direct provision of subsidised social housing is not considered, although it is an important substitute for cash transfers in many countries. The Table shows that most countries operate either a general, means-tested housing-benefit system or offer housing-related supplements in the social-assistance (SA) system. Greece and Spain offer housing-related tax concessions. In the United States, some states offer housing assistance, but there is no Federal system.

Table 8. **Housing support systems**

	Housing support
Australia	income-tested
Austria	-
Belgium	-
Canada	within SA only
Czech Republic	within SA only
Denmark	income-tested + within SA
Finland	income-tested
France	income-tested
Germany	income-tested
Greece	tax allowance
Hungary	income-tested
Iceland	income-tested
Ireland	within SA only
Italy	-
Japan	within SA only
Luxembourg	within SA only
Netherlands	income-tested
New Zealand	income-tested
Norway	within SA only
Portugal	within SA only
Spain	tax credit
Sweden	income-tested
Switzerland	within SA only
United Kingdom	income-tested
United States	-

Source: OECD Database on Taxation and Benefit Entitlements.

The effect of these various schemes on work incentives can be very large. Table 9 assumes that housing costs are 20 per cent of gross earnings in work. It gives the replacement rate for a couple with two children including and excluding housing support. Including housing benefits raises the replacement rate by five percentage points on average, although there is little or no effect in nine countries. The difference is most marked in the United Kingdom, which has the lowest measured replacement rate when housing benefits are excluded, and an above average replacement rate once account is taken of this form of assistance. Denmark, Finland and France also show relatively large differences. In Spain, the tax credit for housing costs marginally reduces the replacement rate because it is worth proportionally more in work than out of work (see the discussion of child-related tax measures above).

Apart from housing support, many other government programmes may determine the level of replacement rates as experienced by families (see section 3.2.2).

Table 9. **Effect of housing support on replacement rates, couple with two children**

Replacement rate (%)	Without housing support	With housing support
Australia	64	71
Belgium	61	61
Canada	66	66
Denmark	73	80
Finland	75	81
France	73	75
Germany	71	79
Ireland	65	65
Italy	47	47
Japan	59	59
Netherlands	71	82
New Zealand	57	64
Norway	73	73
Spain	75	76
Sweden	78	85
Switzerland	84	84
United Kingdom	41	67
United States	60	60

Notes and Source: See Table 2. Replacement rates without housing support are identical to those reported in the last column of Table 7.

3.1.5 *Social assistance benefits and typical net replacement rates*

Social assistance complicates the pattern of employment incentives. The Tables of replacement rates above show the main unemployment benefit, usually unemployment insurance. However, the structure of social assistance benefits often implies higher (net) replacement rates than does unemployment insurance. Table 10 shows the replacement rate from social assistance benefits. Comparing with previous Tables, social assistance is higher than unemployment benefits for couples in Finland, Japan, Norway and Sweden, for example.

Eligibility for social assistance is limited by income and asset tests which in some cases are very restrictive. In Sweden, for example, the social assistance rate suggested by the government (the benefit is administered by local authorities) for a family with two children exceeds the APW level of income. To receive this benefit for more than a short time, all assets must be sold, including owner-occupied housing if alternative rented accommodation is available. Total benefit income from those on social assistance is now capped at 90 per cent of the maximum unemployment insurance entitlement in Denmark after one year. In some other countries social assistance depends on discretionary judgement of need, so replacement rates reported reflect 'typical' rates of payment.

Table 10. **Net replacement rates on social assistance**

Country	Single	Couple no children	Couple 2 children	Single 2 children
Australia	38	50	71	69
Belgium	39	46	59	43
Canada	27	47	54	59
Denmark	65	68	95	90
Finland	61	72	100	70
France	49	57	65	57
Germany	51	59	59	50
Ireland	34	49	70	60
Italy	0	0	11	8
Japan	35	49	72	62
Netherlands	62	74	80	72
New Zealand	41	57	64	55
Norway	46	62	83	64
Spain	27	33	46	44
Sweden	62	83	100	70
Switzerland	49	61	66	57
United Kingdom	52	63	76	65
United States	7	12	49	42

Notes: Calculated on the annualised benefit entitlement in the 60th month of unemployment, assuming that social assistance asset test etc. are satisfied. Replacement rates reflect a strict application of legal provisions rather than common practice if these differ.
Source: see Table 2.

3.1.6   *Replacement rates at different earnings levels*

Insurance benefits are often calculated as being some percentage of previous earnings. Where this is the case, the ratio of in-work to out-of-work incomes will be similar, regardless of the level of earnings which is considered. Insofar as replacement rates do vary, this is due to the operation of the tax system (usually progressive, so net replacement rates after taking account of taxes will be higher the higher are earnings). In contrast, assistance benefits are usually set at a flat rate. Hence the higher are the earnings against which the assistance benefit is compared, the lower will be the replacement rate.

This pattern is reflected in Table 11. In the first month of unemployment (when earnings-related insurance benefits are most likely to be among any benefits received) differences in replacement rates for those with Average Production Workers (APW) earnings, or with 2/3 APW earnings are usually relatively small.[3] The exceptions are those countries with flat-rate payments (Australia, New Zealand, the United Kingdom) or some of those countries where insurance benefits are subject to minimum or maximum payments (Belgium, Denmark). In contrast, after 60 months of unemployment (when generally only assistance benefits will be received) there is a much greater variation in replacement rates at the two different earnings levels.

28

Replacement rates at different earnings' levels can also be affected by income-related benefits paid to those who are working. Benefit supplements to incomes of low-earning families are used to improve work incentives in Australia, Canada, Ireland, Italy, New Zealand (where a new Independent Family Tax Credit was recently announced), the United Kingdom and the United States. These benefits are often focused on families which would otherwise have high replacement rates, particularly families with children. In most cases, the upper earnings limits for eligibility mean that most full-time employees do not receive such benefits. However, they can make a dramatic difference to replacement rates for part-time workers (and in particular for lone parents).[4] Chapter 4 below discusses these benefits in more detail.

Table 11. **Replacement rates at different earnings levels[1]**

	First month of unemployment		60th month of unemployment	
	APW earnings	2/3 APW earnings	APW earnings	2/3 APW earnings
Australia[2,3,4]	71	78	71	78
Belgium	61	**76**	61	91
Canada	66	67	54	61
Denmark[5]	80	95	95	95
Finland	**81**	**89**	100	100
France	75	88	65	83
Germany	79	**77**	59	80
Ireland[3]	65	72	70	72
Italy	47	46	11	14
Japan[3]	**59**	**67**	72	87
Netherlands	82	**84**	80	95
New Zealand[3,4]	64	77	64	77
Norway	**73**	**75**	83	100
Spain	76	73	46	63
Sweden[2,5]	**85**	**85**	100[2]	122[2]
Switzerland	84	**86**	66	91
UK[3]	67	80	76	91
US[6]	60	60	49	42

Notes: In the first month of unemployment it is assumed that families possess enough assets to be ineligible for social assistance. In the 60th month it is assumed that they no longer have such assets and so social assistance (SA) is assumed to be paid where it is higher than other benefits to which they may still be entitled. Figures in **bold** indicate those cases where families would be entitled to SA on the basis of their income, were they not to have been assumed to have been disqualified by an assets test. The replacement rates reflect a strict application of legal provisions rather than common practice, where these differ. Figures in the third column are identical to those in third column of Table 10, except for Belgium (no limitation on the duration of UI effective in this case).

1. It is assumed that the worker is 40 years old, has a dependent spouse and 2 children, and started work at 18. The replacement rates are for the first month of unemployment, after waiting periods have been satisfied. This entitlement is then multiplied by 12 to give an annualised equivalent, on which tax is calculated. The person is fully unemployed. Social assistance is calculated according to a 'typical rate' for the country concerned. Help with housing costs is calculated on the basis of rental costs being 20 per cent of gross APW earnings.
2. Benefit amounts for couples are calculated on the basis of both spouses actively seeking work.
3. Figures for Australia, Ireland, New Zealand and the United Kingdom are for 1995. Unemployment benefit parameters for Japan are for 1996.
4. There is no social insurance in Australia or New Zealand. All figures in the Table, including columns 1-5, refer to the assistance benefit.
5. SA is only available when there is a 'social event' such as unemployment. Low earnings are not themselves a social event.
6. The taxes and benefits are calculated using the rules applying in Detroit, Michigan. All figures include AFDC-UP and Food Stamps.
Source: OECD Database on Taxation and Benefit Entitlements.

3.1.7 *Duration of benefits*

The likelihood of an unemployed person leaving unemployment increases markedly in the period before a fall in benefit entitlement (Atkinson and Micklewright, 1991). But the destination can be either a job or inactivity (including another benefit, such as because of invalidity or early retirement). Benefit systems often have such limited durations. Figure 3 below summarises the major benefit transitions which an unemployed person will face over an eight-year spell of unemployment (for more details on these transitions, see the Seven Country Study, 1996). Unemployment insurance duration often varies by employment record (Germany, Greece, Japan, the Netherlands, Spain and Switzerland) or by age (Austria, Germany,[5] Luxembourg, Portugal), or by family type (Belgium). Furthermore, in practice durations may be more complex than a quick examination of the benefit rules might suggest. In Sweden, benefit entitlement can be renewed by participation in labour market programmes. Similar complications arise in other (especially Nordic) countries. With durations ranging from three months (Japan) to unlimited (Belgian families[6]), the initial replacement rate upon entry into unemployment is an inadequate guide to assess benefit generosity.

3.1.8 *The distribution of work incentives over the population*

Families will take account of the relationship between net incomes in and out of work allowing for all taxes and benefits, not just unemployment benefits, when making work decisions. The tax and benefit system must be considered in its entirety when attempting to assess the differing work incentives facing the working population. Other financial factors in the decision, such as work-related expenses, are discussed below.

One way to take account of tax/benefit interactions is to use microsimulation models. These models indicate how many families are entitled to different combinations of benefits and show how they are taxed (see annex 3). For example, nearly all households receiving unemployment benefit in the United Kingdom also receive housing benefits. The situation is more complicated in the Netherlands, where two-thirds of households receiving social assistance also receive housing benefits, but the equivalent figure for those receiving unemployment insurance is only 12.5 per cent.

Microsimulation models can be used to calculate labour market incentives by comparing the incomes of those currently employed with what they might expect to receive if they became unemployed. The labour market incentives are hypothetical, based on assumptions about what might happen if employed people lose their jobs, or those without jobs find them. Incentives are calculated for the *potential labour force:* all those of working age who are not disabled or in full-time education, including non-working spouses and lone parents. The tax and benefit system can have particularly large disincentive effects on some of the latter groups.

Incentives facing employees

The pattern of incentives found using microsimulation models, summarised in Figure 4, broadly confirms the picture from the hypothetical cases in Tables 2, 5, 7 and 9-11.[7] In Australia and the United States, the most common (individualised -- see annex 1) replacement rate is in the 20 to 40 per cent range. This means that wages after tax are 60 to 80 per cent more than the net benefits they would receive were they unemployed. In Denmark and Sweden, replacement rates are concentrated in the 80 to 100 per cent range. In Germany, Ireland, New Zealand and the United Kingdom, the most common replacement rates are in the range 40 to 60 per cent and in Belgium, Canada, Italy and Norway they are between 60 and 80 per cent. Few workers in any country will benefit financially from moving into unemployment.[8]

Figure 3. **Duration of unemployment benefit entitlements in 1996**

Source: OECD Database on Taxation and Benefit Entitlements.

Chart 4

Distribution of work incentives

Replacement rates of the employed

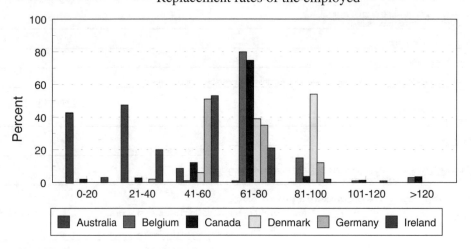

Chart 4 (Cont.)

Distribution of work incentives

Replacement rates of the employed

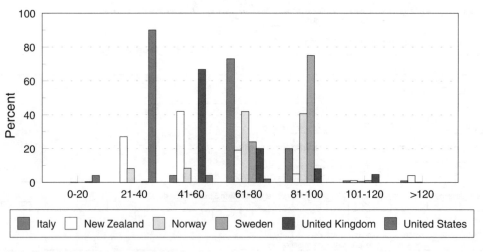

Note: Replacement rates are individualised.
Source: National microsimulation modes: see Annex 3.

Generally, incentives to work tend to be weaker when earnings are lower. Benefits can easily exceed earnings from working part-time, and can also exceed earnings from working full-time for those on very low wages. Few people in employment have replacement rates above 100 per cent, as shown in Figure 4, but this is to be expected as there is no immediate financial return to working. Generally, individuals will only be observed working when replacement rates exceed 100 per cent for non-financial reasons, or to reap longer-term rewards.

Incentives facing those without jobs

If an unemployed person expects to receive a large increase in net income if they started work, they will be more likely to search for employment. The incentive to work, of course, depends on the expected wage. At the median full-time wage, the replacement rate is under 40 per cent for most Australians and Americans who are not currently working; much higher for non-working Danish and Swedish persons, and somewhere in between for other countries. If only low-wage jobs are available (at the lowest decile of earnings), at least a third of people without jobs in Canada and the United States would face replacement rates of over 100 per cent. In Sweden, the proportion of those unemployed with replacement rates below 80 per cent is much higher in the bottom household income decile than for those with higher incomes. This is because unemployment insurance is voluntary. The unemployed who are not covered by insurance receive lower benefits, and so have relatively low replacement rates.

The non-employed group includes both those who are unemployed[9] and those who are not members of the labour force (but excludes those on invalidity and early retirement benefits). Generally, the unemployed face higher replacement rates (and therefore lower work incentives) than others without jobs. For example, two-thirds of the unemployed in Denmark face replacement rates of 80 per cent or more. In Italy, the unemployed have replacement rates of 60 to 80 per cent, whereas others without jobs are found predominantly in the 40 to 60 per cent range. In New Zealand, around half the unemployed have replacement rates of 60 to 80 per cent, whereas others without jobs have lower replacement rates.

Incentives facing different family types

Figure 5 shows how high replacement rates are concentrated on particular family types. If the bar is above the line, a disproportionately large proportion of that family type has replacement rates of over 80 per cent. Of these countries, in Denmark, Germany, Italy and New Zealand there are fewer single people and couples without children with high replacement rates than lone-parent families and couples with children. Weak labour market incentives are concentrated at families with children. Small incentives to work for families with children are a consequence of societies' unwillingness to allow children to grow-up in poverty. In Belgium, Canada, Ireland, Norway, Sweden and the United Kingdom, the pattern is different. Although benefits to families with children in Canada, Ireland and the United Kingdom are higher than for families without children, these countries also provide benefits and tax concessions targeted to families in employment, reducing replacement rates for this group. High replacement rates in Belgium and Norway are concentrated on single people, with or without children. Replacement rates for couples with children are relatively low because the tax system is relatively generous to spouses and dependent children, both when in and out of work.

Chart 5.   **Which family types face strong work disincentives ?**

Over or under representation compared to the average of the country,
of family types facing replacement rates of more than 80%

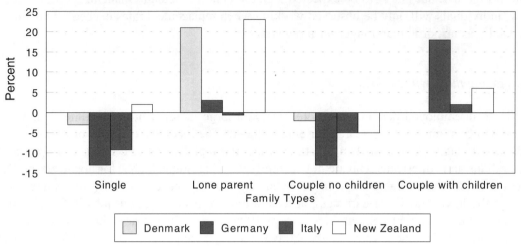

Note: Replacement rates are individualised.
Source: National microsimulation modes: see Annex 3.

Chart 5. (Cont.) **Which family types face strong work disincentives ?**

Over or under representation compared to the average of the country,
of family types facing replacement rates of more than 80%

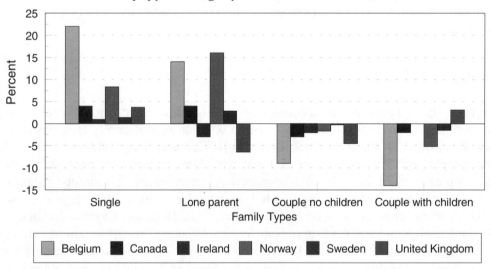

Note: Replacement rates are individualised.
Source: National microsimulation modes: see Annex 3.

Actual replacement rates

The hypothetical replacement rates presented have to assume what happens in the counter-factual case, for example, the earnings an unemployed person might expect to receive. There is relatively little evidence on what happens when people move between employment states. What evidence there is confirms the picture given. Table 12 draws on a study of gains from moving from unemployment to employment in the United Kingdom. Most of the newly employed gained a large amount, but many (especially women) gained relatively little. Looking at the benefit-to-earnings ratio (approximately the same concept as replacement rates), high ratios were predominantly found in families with children.

Table 12. **Distribution of the gap between unemployment-related benefits and net earnings on return to work by sex, United Kingdom.**

Per cent	Men	Women	All
Earnings more than £50 greater than benefit	67	28	56
Earnings £20-50 greater than benefit	23	37	27
Earnings less than £20 greater than benefit	8	30	14
Benefits greater than earnings	3	4	3
Mean difference	£80	£41	£69

Source: Garman, Redmond and Lonsdale (1992), Table 5.4. Average weekly earnings of the sample were £107 per week for men and £84 per week for women.

3.1.9 *Are replacement rates 'too high'?*

The question of whether benefits paid to those out of work are 'too high' or not involves far more considerations than a simple trade-off between economic efficiency and social preferences. Social policy objectives are best served by high levels of benefits, but this can damage the functioning of the labour market. The debate on out-of-work benefits should take many other factors into account.[10]

– **Risk-aversion of workers.** Benefits should be high when people want to insure themselves against loss of earnings arising from unemployment or other risks such as disability. This risk aversion will vary between individuals and over time. The degree of risk aversion may also vary between countries: in some societies people may be more prepared to gamble with their incomes than in others.

– **Relationship between wages and benefit levels.** If benefits are high, wages may be pushed higher as well, increasing the cost of labour and causing unemployment. The responsiveness of wages to out-of-work benefit levels will depend on institutional factors and the degree of competition in labour and product markets.

– **Benefit financing.** High benefit levels require high taxes or social contributions to finance them. If taxes on labour are high, there is a risk that the cost of labour will rise, causing unemployment. This is discussed in more detail in Chapter 5.

– **Job search.** Most people wish to work not just for financial reasons, but because of a strong work ethic, or because of the social interactions work provides. Where this is the case, high replacement rates will not reduce the effort the unemployed put into searching for work. Otherwise, benefit systems attempt to ensure that the unemployed search for work through administrative controls. If these are effective, high replacement rates will not extend the duration of unemployment unduly. Where they are ineffective, some may opt for or adapt to living off benefit income, and not look for work, so increasing unemployment and its persistence.

– **Public employment service.** If public employment services or their private sector equivalents are effective, jobs appropriate to the abilities of the unemployed will be rapidly brought to their attention. Benefits will only need to be sufficient to cover a short period of unemployment as longer job-search will not find better job-offers. If the unemployed have to rely on their own resources in searching for jobs, benefits have to be sufficiently high to support a reasonable length of job-search. Otherwise the unemployed may be forced by financial considerations into accepting inappropriate jobs for their skills; the 'square pegs in round holes' problem.

– **Active labour market policies (ALMPs).** By improving the productivity and employability of the unemployed, active labour market policies can reduce the disincentive effects of any given replacement rate. Conversely, 'If the unemployment benefits system is generous and poorly managed, it is very difficult to operate ALMPs in ways which increase labour market efficiency and reduce structural unemployment' (see Thematic Review of *Enhancing the Effectiveness of ALMPs*).

– **Marginal effective tax rates (METRs).** Increases in earnings may bring very little net increase in family incomes. The result is a reduced incentive to increase earnings. The higher the out-of-work benefit, the higher the METR will have to be and/or the larger the income range over which high METRs apply (see Chapter 4) so deepening or widening this work disincentive.

People may work despite high replacement rates for a number of reasons, including administrative controls social pressures and expectations of higher future wages. But, in the longer term, high replacement rates will tend to undermine work incentives. Systems have been reformed in some countries with the highest replacement rates. In many cases, the main reason for reform has been to curb the high budgetary cost of the programmes concerned, although the subsidiary effect has been to improve work incentives:

– The Netherlands has toughened prior employment requirements for the earnings-related benefit and has tightened eligibility criteria for means-tested benefit receipt;

– Sweden has reduced the unemployment-insurance replacement rate from 80 to 75 per cent of previous earnings;

– The real value of unemployment insurance in Finland has been reduced.

However, some of these apparent reductions in generosity are illusory. Sweden, for example, has eased conditions for regaining eligibility for unemployment insurance following a period out of work. In Finland, as in most other countries, the social assistance benefit can be used to 'top-up' incomes below the social assistance level, and, while unemployment insurance has been reduced, social assistance has not. There was a large rise in the number of social assistance recipients (from 165 000 households in 1989 to 333 000 in 1994). Although higher levels of unemployment amongst those not eligible for insurance benefits and increased take-up as a result of greater awareness of social assistance contributed to this increase, the 'top-up' of the insurance benefit was the main cause. In 1989, 18 per cent of social assistance recipients were also receiving unemployment payments. By 1994, that proportion had risen to 52 per cent. Furthermore, Finland introduced a new benefit (Labour Market Support) to cover those no longer eligible for the main benefit. Benefit reforms must take account of these kinds of system-wide interdependency.

3.2   Other barriers to work rooted in the tax and benefit system

Replacement rates only give a partial picture of incentives to enter employment. Two other factors must be taken into account to get a fuller picture. First, benefits that do not require active job search, such as invalidity and early retirement benefits, may sometimes be used as alternatives to unemployment benefits. Secondly, other aspects of the benefit system than its generosity influence the labour market through effects on the transition from unemployment to employment.

3.2.1.   *Other out-of-work benefits and unemployment benefits*

In many OECD countries more people of working age receive benefits which do not require any job search than are supported by unemployment benefits or covered by active labour market programmes. Recipients of invalidity benefits outnumbered the registered unemployed in 1990 in 12 of the 23 OECD countries for which data are available: Austria, Finland, Greece, Iceland, Italy, Japan, Luxembourg, Netherlands, Norway, Portugal, Sweden and Switzerland. Their number has been growing rapidly, increasing by over 50 per cent since 1980 in Greece, Ireland, Luxembourg, Spain, Sweden and the United Kingdom (Blondal and Pearson, 1995). Along with early retirement schemes, invalidity benefits remove a substantial part of the working-age population from the labour force.

If invalidity benefits were restricted only to those incapable of work, there would be few grounds for concern. However, there is evidence that invalidity and other out-of-work benefits substitute or have substituted for unemployment benefits in some countries as means of supporting those who would otherwise be counted as unemployed. Other benefits are usually unlimited in duration and do not require evidence of job-search. They are also often at a higher level than unemployment benefits. For example, Blondal and Pearson (1995) compare gross invalidity, sickness and early retirement benefits with the index of benefit generosity shown in Figure 2. Under similar assumptions about earnings before receiving benefit, they found replacement rates for the partially disabled were usually much higher than for the unemployed, and for those fully disabled were on average 25 percentage points higher. A range of early-retirement benefits was found to offer even higher replacement rates, especially where beneficiaries had been in employment for a long period before benefit receipt.

For these reasons, it is better from the individual perspective to receive one of these benefits rather than unemployment benefit. Governments reap the political gain from lower headline unemployment rates and employers may find it easier to reduce employment if those losing their jobs receive relatively generous benefits for an unlimited period. Invalidity benefits may be used in this way if medical requirements are not rigidly enforced (either as explicit government policy or by default), as appears to have happened in Austria, Germany, Italy, the Netherlands, Norway, Sweden, and the United Kingdom. A similar trend may be starting in Finland and New Zealand.

Early retirement schemes differ in purpose. Some are merely arrangements whereby individuals can retire early on actuarially reduced pensions. These sorts of early retirement can be justified on the grounds of individuals' control over their own labour-supply or of horizontal equity. More controversial are schemes explicitly designed to remove from the labour force those who might otherwise be unemployed. Such schemes probably will temporarily reduce measured unemployment, but will do nothing to reduce the number of families relying on benefits as their main or only source of income, and -- in the end -- raise overall costs of the social security system. Often, outlays will be even substantially higher, since early retirement benefits tend to be more generous, sometimes substantially so, than are unemployment benefits.

Income support for lone parents raises similar issues. In some countries, such as Sweden, child care is available on demand and all lone parents applying for income support are required to seek work in the same way as other unemployed people. But in many other countries, lone parents are not required to look for work until their youngest child reaches a certain age (16 in Australia and the United Kingdom).

The use of benefits that do not require active job search may lead to complex labour market effects even if the stated intention of these benefits appears to be unrelated to the labour market. In particular, their use as *de facto* unemployment benefits can artificially reduce unemployment rates, without addressing the fundamental causes of unemployment. Furthermore, due account must also be taken of the debilitating effects of families living on benefits, whether unemployment or otherwise. Paying people not to work when they are able to do so is a waste of resources and harmful to the work ethic.

3.2.2   *Incomes and expenses in and out of work*

Cash benefits only account for some of the help given to those who find themselves without jobs. For example, housing benefits may be paid to cover rent or mortgage payments. Some of these benefits are universal, that is, they are not (gradually) withdrawn as income increases. But many benefits will be reduced as family income rises. Although the latter benefits can be included in replacement rate calculations, it is difficult to value other types of help such as provision of social housing. This will only affect incentives if people are required to vacate the housing on finding employment. In contrast, other forms of help may be restricted to those in receipt of benefits (see Table 13). Although some of these are not restricted solely to those on benefits, those in work with low earnings may be less sure of how to claim them or uncertain of their entitlement.

The most substantial of these payments is probably Medicaid in the United States, which covers health care costs for some low-income groups. Since 1991, Medicaid for the 12.1 million recipients of Aid to Families with Dependent Children, AFDC has cost more ($21.9 bn in 1991), than AFDC cash benefits themselves, $20.9 bn (House of Representatives, 1994a). Medicaid is received until AFDC entitlement is exhausted. There is a marginal effective tax rate of substantially more than 100 per cent at the point when Medicaid is exhausted. Extending Medicaid to a broader range of earnings would encourage more AFDC recipients to work. For example, Yelowitz (1995) estimates that if it were possible to earn 25 per cent more than currently without losing Medicaid entitlement, labour force participation would increase by 3.3 percentage points. Furthermore, 14 per cent of the then AFDC caseload would have left AFDC and entered employment. To reduce the disincentive to work resulting from this rule, Medicaid entitlement was extended from 9 to 15 months after losing AFDC.

In Ireland, the value of non-cash benefits -- medicard, butter, footwear and fuel -- is estimated at nearly IR£ 12 per week for a couple with two children. This is equivalent to 10 per cent of the cash transfers received (Department of Enterprise and Employment, 1996). Ireland has a similar provision as Medicaid in the United States whereby the long-term unemployed can continue to receive medical help for three years after taking a new job. The 1996 reforms in New Zealand will increase the qualifying income for a Community Services card by 7.7 per cent, thereby extending benefits to more low-income, in-work families and so smoothing the transition from unemployment to work.

Table 13. **Typical benefits-in-kind which can accrue to those receiving benefits**

Country	Some of the items which can be made available to those on benefit income
Australia	Health care card (reduced cost medicines). Public and private providers sometimes use the card as a passport for other concessions of which reduced transport cost is the most important. School uniforms, books, help with utility payments are given in some states. (Benefit recipients get these cards as of right; low-earning households can get them on application)
Canada	Clothing, health premiums, prescriptions, dental, optical (varies by province), educational costs, removal costs. For example, Ontario pays a winter clothing allowance of $104, and a 'back-to-school' allowance of $126. Six out of 10 Provinces give these benefits to those on low wages as well.
Denmark	Medical expenses.
Finland	Various one-off payments. Health care costs sometimes covered.
Germany	Medical insurance, prescriptions, lower price public services.
Ireland	Back-to -school allowance. Free school meals/transport. Fuel allowance. Medicard.
Japan	Exempted from inhabitants tax (local tax). Cheap rail travel.
Luxembourg	Free transport. Medical insurance
New Zealand	Health-care costs (including prescriptions). Available to all those with low incomes, not just benefit recipients.
Norway	Municipal services (child care, *etc.*) are often income related.
Spain	Health insurance.
Sweden	Prescription costs, glasses, dental.
UK	(if on income support): cold-weather payments; school meals; prescriptions; optical and dental. Other people on low incomes must apply for some of these payments.
US	Medical insurance (Medicaid)

Source: Eardley *et al.* (1996); OECD calculations.

Apart from loss of benefits which are available to those without work, there are increased costs for those in work. These may include commuting expenses, the costs of special clothing and tools, trade union dues and child-care. Garman *et al.* (1992) found that two-thirds of the unemployed in the United Kingdom reported average travel-to-work costs of nearly 7 per cent of earnings. Of the unemployed moving into a job, 18 per cent reported increased expenses, mainly one-off, 'back-to-work' costs, such as for tools or clothing.

Conversely, the unemployed may have out-of-work expenses -- such as job search costs -- which are not incurred in work. In the United Kingdom, four-fifths of the unemployed reported regular job-search expenses averaging £5 (US$8) per week (Garman *et al., 1*992). Typical weekly search costs are IR£6.40 (US$11) in Ireland (Department of Enterprise and Employment, 1996).

Fourteen OECD countries report deductions for work-related expenses in the personal income tax (OECD, 1995*c*) at the earnings level of the average production worker (see below for a discussion of child-care), although they vary enormously in value, see Table 14. Since the unemployed have no access to this deduction, it tends to reduce replacement rates, and to increase the incentive to work.

Table 14.   **Personal income tax deductions for work-related expenses, employees at the earnings of the average production worker, 1994**

Country	Annual allowance for work-related expenses	
	National currency	Per cent APW earnings
Australia	1 100	3.2
Austria	1 800	0.6
Belgium	66 518	7.7
Denmark	3 553	1.6
Finland	2 100	1.7
France	8 422	7.3
Germany	2 000	3.7
Ireland	36	0.3
Luxembourg	36 600	3.7
Netherlands	2 086	3.8
Norway	28 100	13.9
Spain	97 344	5.0
Switzerland	1 700	2.9
United Kingdom	11	0.1

Source: OECD (1995c).

Some countries -- Belgium, Denmark, Finland, Germany, the Netherlands and Switzerland and the United States -- also have specific rules relating to the deductibility of commuting expenses. Although the cost of providing such deductions is difficult to assess, tax expenditure accounts give an indication. In France, for example, identifiable revenues foregone for work-related expenses in 1992 (see Ministère des Finances, 1993) include:

– contributions to trades unions (FF 190m, US$40m);

– child-care costs (FF 1 bn, US$200 m for the purchase of such care and providers also receive concessions on the social contributions they are required to make);

– food vouchers or work canteens (FF 650 m, US$130 m);

– holiday vouchers (FF 25m, US$5 m); and

– transport costs (FF 255m, US$50 m).

As these data on revenues foregone indicate, child-care costs are often the most substantial in-work expense. They are commonly identified as a barrier to taking employment, especially for lone-parent families or when one partner is already working. Public policies to provide access to affordable child-care facilities for parents who wish to work are many but diverse (see Ergas, 1990, for a summary). Publicly-provided day-care facilities may be subsidised by central or local government, with only nominal charges to users.

Other countries, including Belgium, Canada, the Netherlands, New Zealand and Norway allow some or all of expenses on formal child-care to be deducted from personal income tax liabilities.[11] Although administratively straightforward, these deductions may be worth more to individuals or households subject to higher tax rates, and be worth nothing for those earning wages below the tax threshold. They have little effect on replacement rates of the low-paid.

Table 15.   **Child-care costs and benefits: a barrier to work?**
Percentage gain in net income from work taking account of child-care costs and benefits

Gain in income from work (%)	Child-care cost assumption	2/3 APW earnings			APW earnings		
	1	2	3	4	5	6	7
	$ per week	Ignoring child-care costs and benefits	After child-care costs for those in work	After child-care costs and benefits for those in work	Ignoring child-care costs and benefits	After child-care costs for those in work	After child-care costs and benefits for those in work
Australia	167 (max)	28	-27	-1	41	-25	-5
	75	28	-21	3	41	-19	0
Canada	140 (max)	50	5	20	50	18	45
	75	50	3	18	50	15	43
Finland	(145)[1]	15	-43	15	116	-32	16
Japan[2]	(242)[1]	108	50	108	138	92	115
United Kingdom[3]	60 (max)	27	-2	50	54	27	30
	75	27	-10	45	54	21	24

Notes: In columns 2 and 5 child-care costs and benefits are ignored. In Columns 3, 4, 6 and 7 it is assumed that when in work the costs in column 1 must be incurred. When unemployed the family is assumed not to use child-care facilities (see text for a discussion of the treatment of child care for the unemployed). The Table gives the percentage increase in net income compared with that which would be received when in the first month of unemployment. In Australia, Canada and the United Kingdom, two cases are included in the Table. The maximum level of child-care costs which will qualify for help may be above typical child-care costs, so the effects of having costs of $75 per week are illustrated. The gains in net income are calculated for a one-earner couple with two children (except in the United Kingdom, where the benefit provision applies only to lone-parents). The pattern of incentives for other family types closely follows that in the Table; the case of a one-earner couple is included as this family type is discussed in more detail in Tables 2, 5, 7, 9, and 10. .

1.   In Finland and Japan, payments for child care are made according to income. There is therefore no underlying child-care cost. The figure here refers to the maximum that would be paid for two children. In each country, this amount would only be paid by someone with substantially more than average earnings. Columns 3 and 6 refer to the net gain in income were the family to pay the maximum amount as opposed to the amount relevant for someone with their income level.

2.   The figures here reflect payments in the Osaka municipality.

3.   A lone-parent family where the Family-Credit hours' rule has been satisfied.

Source: OECD Database on Taxation and Benefit Entitlements.

Table 15 serves to underline the fact that child-care costs can be a serious barrier to enter work. Columns 2 and 5 show the gain in net income a one-earner couple receives from working compared with being unemployed (it reflects the first-month unemployment assumption of Tables 5,

7, 9 and 10 including all benefits). At both APW and 2/3 APW earnings, there is a clear financial gain from working in all the countries included in the table. Columns 3 and 6 show the gain in net income if the child-care costs of column 1 are taken into account (it is assumed that child care is bought only when employed). Work no longer brings financial reward; on the contrary, in most of the cases in Table 4, the family would be better off remaining on benefits than to go to work. Columns 4 and 7 show that special provisions in tax and benefit systems can reduce substantially the barriers to work from child-care costs.

Such barriers will be particularly important where informal arrangements for child care are unavailable, in particular for lone-parent families and families where both earners wish to work. These family types were not included in Table 15 in order to retain comparability with the single-earner family cases discussed in more detail in this chapter. However, the size of the barriers to work caused by child-care costs are similar to those indicated in Table 15. Lone-parents and second-earners are two of the groups which most estimates suggest are particularly responsive to financial incentives to work. Some estimates claim large effects on the employment of these groups arising from measures to promote child care. Australia has increased the level of support for child care through subsidising provision and through cash rebates and benefits. In the United Kingdom, up to £40 per week of child-care costs can now be disregarded when determining benefit receipt. It is estimated that 40 000 extra lone parents will work as a result of this change in the rules (Duncan, Giles and Webb, 1994). New Zealand also offers a disregard to lone parents with child-care costs (along with a general income-tested child-care subsidy).

However, if child-care charges, benefits or tax rebates are related to income or employment status, there is an additional element built into the tax and benefit system which reduces the supply of labour. For example, Finland pays child-home-care allowance to parents who do not use the public kindergartens for children under three years of age.[12] If child care outside the home has to be used when work is found, the financial costs of work include the loss of the allowance. Elsewhere, the effect of withdrawing benefits and tax rebates as incomes rise is to increase the marginal effective tax rate, so blunting the incentive facing all those already working to provide more labour (see Chapter 4).

It is unrealistic to treat child-care costs solely as a work expense. This ignores the private and social benefits of child-care provision. Child-care is often consumed independently of whether parents work or not and in some countries child-care services are available to make time available for job search. Government policy in Sweden is that those on social assistance should continue to use child-care for this reason.

3.2.3   Cash-flow and the transition to work

Even where there is an apparent financial benefit in becoming employed, the short-term consequences may be the opposite. For households which are (almost by definition) short of money, this may appear to the families concerned an almost unassailable barrier to taking a job. The cash-flow consequences of taking employment can be unfortunate if there is a hiatus in public support. For example, several countries have one system of supporting those who are unemployed and another which supplements the income of those who have low earnings. In some cases, they are administered by different agencies, causing co-ordination problems. The transition from one benefit regime to another can lead to delays in payment, causing severe hardship to the families in question and discouraging attempts to move off benefit.

Transitional problems are likely to be of most consequence in countries with low benefit levels. This has been identified as a problem in the United Kingdom, where a commitment has been made to process all claims for the employment-conditional Family Credit within a maximum of two days. In the United States, the Earned Income Tax Credit gives a substantial boost to in-work incomes (see below). But it may have had a limited labour-supply impact in practice because it is generally paid annually when tax returns are filed, rather than throughout the year when it would have most impact. In New Zealand, some out-of-work benefits will continue to be paid for a period until in-work benefits are granted, with an end-of-year reconciliation. In Australia, unemployment benefits are paid two weeks in arrears, meaning that benefits will continue to be received for a short period when moving into work.

"Back-to-work bonuses" have a similar effect. Not only would they help the transition to employment, but they can also be structured to encourage job search. Such a system is in place in Japan, where the more rapidly an unemployed person finds a job, the larger is the bonus paid, up to a maximum equal to 4 months of benefit. Some long-term unemployed in Australia receive a payment of A\$ 100 on entry into employment. New Zealand pays NZ\$ 250 towards the back-to-work expenses of those who find work after a year or more of unemployment. Experiments with similar schemes in the United States suggest that they encouraged enough benefit recipients to find jobs more quickly than they otherwise would have done, for the scheme to more than cover its costs.

The tax system can also reduce the cash-flow returns to working. In several OECD countries, personal income tax is withheld from earnings at source at a rate which will approximate to the year-end, annual tax liability. If someone enters employment after a period of receiving benefit, there may be an over-retention of earnings at source in a progressive tax system. There may eventually be a repayment of the excess tax paid, but in the mean time the cash-constrained individual has in effect been obliged to give a loan to the government.

3.2.4   *Uncertainty and the transition to work*

The calculations above imply that a replacement rate can be identified for individuals and they will respond in a predictable way to the resultant incentives. However, calculating the net incomes of someone in and out of work, taking account of family allowances, earnings additions, peculiarities of the tax system, the interactions of benefits, and the timing of payments, requires knowledge of many pages of regulations. Small wonder, then, that surveys suggest people have very little idea of how much net income they might have were they to move from being employed to unemployed, or vice versa. For example, in reviewing changes in Australia, researchers concluded that 'The majority of respondents were largely unaware of how the income test works and the effect that earning income had on their allowance or pension...the impact of social income tests tends to be misinterpreted in that they are generally viewed as being harsher than they actually are' (Puniard and Harrington, 1993). In the United Kingdom, the employment-conditional Family Credit is not widely understood; many recipients underestimate how much they might be able to earn without exhausting their rights to the benefit (Marsh and McKay, 1993).

This lack of understanding about the benefit system and incomes which can be expected in and out of work has three possible effects. First, when combined with the effects of the administrative burden placed on claimants, the take-up of certain key benefits may be too low. Low take-up has historically been a particular problem with benefits paid to those on low incomes *in*-work. Hence provisions of the benefit system which in theory should have positive effects on the incentive

43

to work, in practice may have a lesser effect. Secondly, misperceptions of net incomes in and out of work may lead people to behave irrationally. In theory, the effects of misconceptions on employment are unclear. People might over- or under-estimate net incomes in employment or unemployment. However, knowledge of in-work benefits is often more limited than is awareness of out-of-work benefits, which is part of the reason for the low take-up of such benefits. There can be a presumption that this leads people to overestimate replacement rates, with potentially negative effects on the labour market. Thirdly, lack of knowledge adds to the uncertainty surrounding incomes in work as opposed to incomes out of work. Taking a job involves assessing the values of a host of unknown variables -- work expenses, tax bills, benefit entitlements[13] -- which those without jobs are unable to gauge with much accuracy. Complex administrative procedures add to the perception that actual benefit receipts are something of a lottery. The requirement to reapply for benefits if any job is lost again implies that families must throw themselves on the mercy of an ill-understood and apparently arbitrary system, so discouraging the acceptance of 'risky' jobs.[14] An Australian study concluded in language which echoes findings of other studies: 'work decisions of benefit recipients are also influenced by the way benefits are administered and the penalties this imposes (sometimes inadvertently) on those considering re-entering the labour force. Where administrative procedures are cumbersome and time-consuming, or where the rules themselves discourage benefit re-application (for example, by imposing waiting periods), the perceived risks of accepting a job can offset any potential gain in income' (Saunders, 1995).

The uncertainty over incomes in and out of work is caused by a lack of transparency in tax and benefit systems. Transparency could be increased by simplifying the tax and benefit system. Short of this, there are several other policy options which have been tried in different OECD countries. Information campaigns in the United Kingdom have had a dramatic effect on take-up of Family Credit, the main employment-conditional benefit. Several countries have identified a particular problem with the long-term unemployed being unaware of net incomes in work, and attempt to target information campaigns on them. Employers may be a source of advice to prospective employees when job-offers are made, so it is important that they too understand the tax and benefit system.[15]

3.3   Policy responses to promote employment

Although the effects of replacement rates on unemployment are relatively uncontroversial in sign, it is often questioned whether the social cost is a price worth paying. General reforms to reduce replacement rates have therefore been rare (see Box 1). Most recent reforms have usually been targeted. Reforms in Denmark in 1994 and 1995 restricted the maximum amount of social assistance compared with lost earnings[16] and the period over which high levels of social assistance can be received. Maximum rates of housing benefit in the United Kingdom will be reduced.[17] In addition, some countries have up-rated their benefits or the minima and maxima in the insurance benefits in line with price inflation rather than earnings. This led to a slight increase in replacement rates around 1992-1993, as real earnings fell, but this approach has more often led to lower replacement rates (for example in the United Kingdom). Young people have been the focus of a more general international trend, with removal of rights to benefit of 16 to 17 year olds in Canada and New Zealand, restrictions on the amount of benefit in the Netherlands and the duration of benefits for young people in Denmark.[18] Many of these reforms were introduced for budgetary reasons as well as due to concerns about work incentives.

Besides cutting the replacement rate, reforms have concentrated on other aspects of policy mentioned in Box 2 or recommended in the *Jobs Study* (OECD, 1994*a* and 1995*b*). For example,

– *Reinforcing the insurance principle.* This has taken various forms. Some countries are looking to reduce heavy individual use of the unemployment insurance system. Canada is considering a reform which would reduce entitlements to those who repeatedly become unemployed; Austria is considering experience-rating employers' social security contributions to reflect the numbers they lay-off. Other countries are reducing entitlements to unemployment insurance benefits (Belgium and Norway have reformed unemployment insurance for part-time work; longer contribution periods before receipt of unemployment insurance benefits are now required in Sweden). In Finland, access to the basic unemployment insurance for those without work experience was restricted in 1994, with a new means-tested benefit introduced for those who no longer qualify. In the Netherlands, access to wage-related benefit has been tightened so that 26 out of the last 39 weeks and four out of the past five years must have been worked. Required contribution periods were increased in Spain in 1992.

– *Encouraging job search.* Belgium has tightened administration of the requirement to search for work. As a result 35 000 people lost their unemployment insurance entitlements in 1993. A similar tightening of administration has recently taken place in Denmark and the United Kingdom. In the Netherlands, 90 000 recipients of unemployment insurance were 'sanctioned' in 1993, compared with around 40 000 just three years before. In 1996, more detailed proof of job-search activity was required to gain access to the means-tested benefit in the Netherlands. One other way in which job search can be enforced is done is through use of active labour market policies (see OECD, 1996*c*). Job-search requirements were tightened in Spain in 1992.

– *Improving access to child-care.* Some countries with relatively poor records in providing child-care have recently focused more attention on this area. In Australia, child-care costs are refunded in part according to parental income, suppliers are subsidised and a third of remaining expenditures is granted a cash rebate. Some families pay as little as A\$ 19 for a full week of child care (12 per cent of the cost of provision). Government expenditures on child care now amount to A\$ 1 bn (12 percent of expenditure on unemployment benefits). The United Kingdom has increased the amount of earnings which are disregarded for expenditure on child care, and has started a programme giving vouchers to all parents of young children which can be used to purchase nursery school places.

– *Increasing in-work incomes.* Tax reductions for those on low incomes can increase net incomes in work, although the effect on replacement rates depends on the tax treatment of benefits and the financing of the tax reduction. An area of tax and benefit policy which has received much more attention is the payment of benefits or income tax credits on condition that the recipient is in employment. But they raise another labour market problem, that of high marginal effective tax rates, which is considered next.

Chapter 4

THE POVERTY TRAP AND HIGH MARGINAL EFFECTIVE TAX RATES (METRs)

4.1   What causes high METRs?

If benefits are withdrawn as soon as earnings rise above zero, there is a severe disincentive to work -- the unemployment trap is severe. Countries withdraw benefits as earnings rise sometimes on a one-for-one basis, sometimes more gradually. In many countries a significant number of people with earnings continue to receive benefits even while they are paying taxes and social contributions. The rates at which benefits are withdrawn and taxes increase as earnings rise is known as the marginal effective tax rate (METR). People facing very high METRs have little or no financial reward for increased work hours and effort, and lose very little if they work less. METRs can be lowered by cutting the benefit reduction rate (BRR), but only at the cost of extending benefit entitlements further up the income distribution.

Examples of high METRs and their causes are indicated in Table 16 below. Many of the examples of high METRs arise from the policy towards families (as in Australia, Germany, Ireland, the United Kingdom and the United States). Child tax allowances and universal child benefits are paid in most OECD countries but the budgetary cost means that the amounts transfered are usually not very high. In those countries where unemployment benefit levels are low, such payments are insufficient to prevent child poverty, and as a result additional child payments are sometimes made to families receiving benefits. To avoid the sudden loss of income on entering employment referred to above, two policies have been followed. In some countries, including Australia, Germany and New Zealand, the family payment is withdrawn gradually as income rises (although the means tests for family payments were eliminated in Germany in 1996). In Ireland and the United Kingdom, a separate benefit is paid to families in employment, which again is withdrawn as incomes increase. In each case, the withdrawal of the benefit leads to high METRs. Furthermore, the treatment of child-care costs can increase METRs to even higher levels than indicated in Table 16.

High METRs are more general, both in these and other countries, than Table 16 suggests. Payments which are means-tested on family income often are reduced by the amount of all other income -- the METR is 100 per cent. In such circumstances it is sometimes said that recipients face a poverty trap -- any attempt to increase earnings has no effect on household income (see below). The number of people not entitled to insurance benefits has risen, increasing the reliance on means-tested benefits. This stems both from people who have exhausted their unemployment insurance benefits, and those who have never worked and so have never contributed to unemployment insurance schemes. Some of the more dramatic increases are noted in Table 17 below. In addition, most special benefits for lone-parent families are means-tested.

Table 16. Incidence and causes of high marginal effective tax rates
(One-earner couples)

	METR	Region where METR applies (% of APW earnings)	Tax and benefit combinations causing high METRs
Australia	90%	38-62%	Income tax (20%), Parenting allowance (70%)
	38%	62-78%	Income tax (34%), low-income rebate withdrawal (4%)
	104%	78-84%	Income tax (34%), Medicare payments (20%), Additional family payment (50%)
	85%	84-100%	Income tax (34%), Additional Family Payment (50%), Medicare levy (1.45%)
France	78%	57-91%	RMI disregard (50%), social security (18.7%), CSG (2.3%), Housing Benefit (16.5% average)
Germany	89%	72-82%	Milderungszone (phase out of income-tax free zone (this has now been abolished)): income tax (51%), social security (18.3%), housing benefit (20%)
Ireland	105.5%	62-76%	Social Security (5.5%), Income tax (40%), Family Income Supplement (60%)
Sweden	72%	147-160%	Income Tax (20%), social security contributions(2%), local tax (31%), Housing Benefit (20%)
UK	97%	46-65%	Income Tax (20%), social security(10%), Family Credit (70%), Housing Benefit (65%) Council Tax Benefit (20%)
	80.5%	65-77%	Income Tax (25%), social security(10%), Family Credit (70%)
US	72%	62-71%	Social Security (7.65%), Income Tax (15%), Local Tax (5%), Food Stamps (24%), Earned Income Tax Credit (17.68% for family with two children).

Notes: 1994 systems except for Australia and the United Kingdom (1995). Family Credit is only revised every six months, so the long term METR given in the Table for the United Kingdom may be substantially higher than that faced in the short term. Fewer than half of Ireland's Family Income Supplement recipients are on earnings' levels that are exposed to the METR indicated. The benefit level, once set, is not revised downwards for 12 months even if income increases in the meantime. The long-term rate presented in the Table is substantially higher than that faced in the short term. Figures for individual taxes and benefits do not sum to the overall METR in the United Kingdom because benefits are withdrawn against net rather than gross income. The 38% rate for Australia is included to give a better impression of Australian METRs.
Source: OECD Database on Taxation and Benefit Entitlements.

Table 17. Growth in receipt of means-tested benefits, 1980-1992

	1980	1985	1990	1992	index
Austria (unemployment assistance)	6 000	74 000	64 000	58 000	967
Belgium (Minimex)	25 135[1]	43 774[2]	48 895	63 232[3]	252
Canada (social assistance)	734 300[1]	1 058 000	1 056 000	1 675 900[3]	228
Finland (social assistance)(number of persons)	168 000	240 000	314 000	577 000[3]	343
France (RMI)	-	-	510 145	792 944[4]	-
Germany (Sozialhilfe)	1 322 000	2 063 000	2 890 000	3 649 000	276
Germany (Unemployment assistance)	122 000	670 000	433 000		-
Netherlands (RWW - Unemployment assistance)	105 000	396 800	335 900	314 700	300
Spain (Assistance benefit)	105 971	595 884	616 159	728 342[5]	687
Sweden (social assistance) (number of persons)	343 329	535 557	515 285	715 212	208
United Kingdom (income support, excluding disabled or over age 60)	1 225 000	2 919 000[2]	2 175 000	3 020 000	247
United States (Food Stamps)	1 920 000	1 990 000	2 000 000	2 660 000[4]	139

Notes: Number of households except where noted otherwise. The French RMI was introduced in 1989. Figures for United Kingdom are for supplementary benefit in 1980 and 1986.
1. 1981
2. 1986
3. 1994
4. 1993
5. 1991
Source: Eardley *et al.* (1996).

4.2. Who faces high METRs?

High METRs are not restricted to those countries where means-testing has traditionally played an important role in the benefit system. For example, Germany is a country which has an extensive insurance system, but also has a variety of means-tested benefits. Table 18 gives the distribution of METRs in Germany by family type. The Table shows the proportion of people who, if their earned income increased by 100 DM, would experience a METR in the ranges given. Four per cent face a marginal rate over 100 per cent (that is, an extra unit of earnings makes them worse off), and a further 11 per cent face a marginal rate between 60 and 100 per cent. In New Zealand, only around four per cent of the potential labour force face METRs greater than 60 per cent. The equivalent figure in the United States is less than two per cent. Table 19 gives the distribution of marginal tax rates among the employed population for a range of countries (note that Table 18 covers the whole potential labour force including unemployed and non-employed).

Table 18.   **Distribution of marginal effective tax rates by family type, Germany, 1993**
(percentage of families)

Marginal effective tax rate (percentage of gross earnings)	Single person	Lone-parent family	Married couple without children	Married couple with children	Total
0-20	1	7	3	4	4
21-40	20	17	50	57	41
41-60	58	31	40	29	40
61-80	5	13	2	4	5
81-100	9	21	1	2	6
over 100	7	11	4	4	4
Total	100	100	100	100	100

Notes: METRs are calculated for the potential labour force. This includes the actual labour force (employed and unemployed) and the non-employed population of working age who are neither students nor in receipt of benefits which preclude work, such as early-retirement and disability pensions. METR estimates are highly sensitive to the assumption made about the marginal unit of income involved. Most means-tested benefits have an earnings disregard, so the METR is zero.
Source: See annex 3.

Table 19.   **Distribution of marginal effective tax rates of the employed population**

Per cent of workers	1-20	21-40	41-60	61-80	81-100	100+
Australia	3.4	58.9	34.0	1.2	2.0	0.5
Finland	1.8	12.4	77.7	6.9	1.0	0.2
Germany	4.0	41.0	40.0	5.0	6.0	4.0
Italy	4.8	3.9	69.4	21.8	0.0	0.0
New Zealand	15.6	72.5	8.3	1.1	2.0	0.5
Sweden	0.0	4.0	80.0	12.0	2.0	2.0
United Kingdom	13.9	74.5	4.6	2.3	1.4	2.7

Notes: METRs calculated only for those with earnings because data on the unemployed and non-employed are not comparable between countries. Annex 3 describes the sources of the estimates. See also notes to Table 18.
Source: See annex 3.

These figures should not be interpreted as a guide to the severity of the effects of high METRs. High METRs over a range of earnings imply that there is very little incentive to earn in that range. For example, someone facing a 100 per cent METR could reduce hours of work and earnings without affecting their net income. If people respond to these incentives, few will be observed working with high METRs. The effect on the labour market may be large if many people reduce their labour supply in response.

Although the numbers of individuals and households facing high METRs vary from country to country, some patterns are clear. More women than men are affected by high METRs. In both New Zealand and the United States, there are more than twice as many women facing METRs of over 60 per cent than there are men, and a similar pattern is observed in the Netherlands. Furthermore, the higher level of benefits payable for children implies that means-testing continues higher up the earnings scale, affecting more people. Unsurprisingly, therefore, in nearly every OECD country for which there is information, the group most affected by high METRs are lone parents. Table 18 shows 45 per cent of German lone parents have METRs over 60 per cent compared with only 15 per cent of the total potential labour force. Twenty-four per cent of female lone parents in New Zealand face marginal rates of over 60 per cent; and in the United Kingdom over 65 per cent of lone parents with earnings have similarly high METRs.

4.3   High METRs and the labour market

Sometimes, it is argued that the importance of high METRs is exaggerated. Most labour market decisions are not 'marginal' in the sense of working only a few more hours, or trying to earn a slightly higher wage. Instead they consist of large, discrete changes in status -- from not working to working full-time. These views may be justified where high METRs exist for only a short range of earnings, since these are unlikely to distort labour market behaviour. But there are cases where high METRs do matter. Where marginal rates are high over a relatively wide range of earnings they break the link between effort and reward, which reduces work incentives.[19] One of the many country-specific examples which could be quoted here concerns elderly workers in Japan. Beyond the age of 60, pensions could be combined with earnings. If earnings were relatively low, they could be combined with 80 per cent of the full pension. Beyond a certain threshold of earnings, the amount of pension would be reduced to 60 per cent of the full pension. As a result, earnings of those entitled to a pension were highly concentrated just below the earnings level which would result in a big loss of pension. No such pattern was observed for those with no pension entitlement. People apparently do respond to the incentives facing them (Seike, 1994, Seike and Shimada, 1995) and the Japanese authorities have responded by reforming this system.

The other area where high METRs have a strong impact on the labour market is when they affect the most disadvantaged groups. The specific problems of lone parents were noted above. Social assistance recipients often face METRs of 100 per cent. The consequence is that it is not possible in these circumstances to increase disposable income unless a full-time job can be found. Thus, tax and benefit systems can interact to prevent formal part-time work, and thereby encourage fraud and long-term benefit dependency. Some countries which have faced this problem have reduced METRs below 100 per cent to permit limited part-time work. METRs are particularly important in three policy areas; the poverty trap, the use of employment-conditional taxes and benefits (often called 'in-work benefits'), and the taxation of the family.

50

4.4　The poverty trap

Two problems arise in the application of means-tests to families receiving social assistance. First, after work-related expenses, the family can find itself with *reduced* disposable income if one member undertakes low-paid or part-time work. This is a 'poverty trap': income is low, but a few hours of work might leave them worse off than relying on benefits as the sole source of family income. In the absence of full-time work, such families are discouraged from any contact with the labour market. Lack of contact with the labour market over a sustained period reduces the effectiveness with which people can search for jobs, while there is an increasing risk that employers will regard such individuals as 'unemployable'. A study of AFDC recipients in the United States concludes that after taking account of work expenses, METRs can be more than 100 per cent, with 'pernicious' effects (Giannarelli and Steuerle, 1994).

The second problem is that the incentive for one member of the family to work can be affected by the labour market position of the other. The earnings of one spouse reduce the benefit entitlement of the other. This has long been recognised as a problem in countries with extensive means-testing, such as Australia and the United Kingdom (see Scherer, 1977). In Australia, 65 per cent of women married to employed men are working, compared with 26 per cent of those married to men who are unemployed or out of the labour force (Bradbury, 1995). The position is similar in the United Kingdom, with 74 per cent of women married to employed men working, compared with 33 per cent of women married to men not in jobs (Office of Population Censuses and Surveys, 1995). Longitudinal studies, which track the labour market experience of husband and wife during an unemployment spell, paint a similar picture. Garman *et al.* (1992) found that just 26 per cent of women married to newly unemployed men were working 9 months later if their husband was continuously unemployed over the period, compared with 47 per cent if he found work at some time in the interim. Other longitudinal studies confirm this finding.[20]

Disincentives in the benefit system are not the sole cause of the strong correlation between spouses' employment. Spouses usually have similar educational profiles and, of course, are usually searching for jobs in the same local labour market. A recent Australian study concluded 'variations in the characteristics of married women distinguished according to the employment status of their partner are sufficient to explain almost all of the variation in employment rates between these groups of women' (Bradbury, King and McHugh, 1996).

However, other econometric analyses, controlling for characteristics which might explain wives' participation rates, suggest that the shortfall in employment rates of women married to unemployed men cannot always be explained by these factors alone. In the United Kingdom, Kell and Wright (1990) find a 39 per cent shortfall and Davies, Elias and Penn (1992) a 10 to 20 per cent shortfall that could be directly attributed to the husband's unemployment.

This pattern -- low participation by wives of unemployed men -- is increasingly observed in other countries as greater numbers receive means-tested benefits.[21] In the Netherlands, Kersten *et al.* (1993) found strong disincentives resulting from the benefit system affecting women married to men in receipt of a means-tested benefit, even after adjusting for the characteristics of the wife. In Germany, there is a large difference in the working patterns of women married to unemployed men according to the benefit which the family is receiving. Of women married to men receiving unemployment assistance benefits, just 28 per cent are working compared with 41 per cent of those whose husbands receive unemployment insurance. In cases where the husband is unemployed but receiving *neither* benefit, 71 per cent of wives are working (Giannelli and Micklewright, 1995).

Table 20. **Employment-conditional tax credits and benefits**

	Canada	Ireland	Italy	New Zealand	United Kingdom	United States
Name	Child tax benefit	Family income supplement	Family benefits for employees[1]	Independent Family Tax Credit (to be introduced)	Family credit	Earned income tax credit
Cost	C$ 250m =$200m	IR£21.3m =$33.9m	Lit 5763 bn = $3.76 bn	NZ$ 210m	£1 1 bn =$1.7 bn	$26.7 bn
Number of recipients	0.7m	11 000	-	150 000	0.5m	19m
Average receipt	C$ 357	IR£1 925 =$3 075	-	NZ$ 27	£2 400 =$3 800	$1 450
Responsible department	Tax administration	Social security	Social security	Tax administration	Social security	Tax administration
Maximum benefit	C$ 500pa	[2]	Lit 2.76 m pa	NZ$ 15pw per child	£67.80pw[3]	$2 152/3 556/ 323 pa
Minimum earnings	C$ 3 750	none	[4]		none	$0
Phase in rate	8%	none	none		none	34/40/7.65%
Earnings when phasing out begins	C$ 20 921	immediately	Lit 15.984m		£73pw	$11 610/11 610/ 5 280 pa
Withdrawal rate	10% of gross income	60% of gross income	10% of gross income	18% between NZ$ 20 000 and NZ$ 27 000, 30% above[5]	70% of net income	16.0/21.1/7.7% of gross income
Minimum hours worked	no limit	20 (19 hours from July 1996) hours	no limit[6]		16 hours. Supplement for 30 hours or more	no limit
Family type	Families with children	Families with children[7]	Families receiving unemployment benefit[8]		Families with children. Pilot scheme for childless	First figure is for 1 child families, 2nd for 2 or more children, 3rd for no children

Notes: Data on the entitlement rules refer to 1995 except for New Zealand (IFTC, 1997) and the United States (1996). Data on costs, number of recipients *etc.* refer to 1993 for Canada and Ireland, 1990 for Italy and 1994 for the United Kingdom and United States. IFTC figures for New Zealand are forecasts for when the scheme is fully implemented in 1998-99. The pre-existing Guaranteed Minimum Family Income, which is a smaller employment-conditional payment, will continue to be paid. The GMFI is paid to lone parents working more than 20 hours and couples working more than 30 hours. The maximum benefit is around NZ110 per week. The difference between family income and NZ$ 320 is paid. As all eligible families receive family benefits, and there is a minimum wage of around NZ$ 6.25 per hour, maximum benefit for lone parents is around NZ$ 110, substantially less (around NZ$ 30) for single-earner couples. It has approximately 5 000 recipients. It is operated through the tax administration. Figures for the EITC are total programme costs including the outlay on repayments and the tax expenditure component (the reduction in tax liabilities).

1. In addition to this payment, Italy has income-related tax credits for dependent spouses and children.
2. Payment is 60% of the difference between family income before tax and a weekly threshold of IR£165 plus IR£20 per child with a minimum payment of £5.
3. Rates depend on age and number of children. The above figure is for 2 children aged under 11.
4. Ordinary unemployment benefit only lasts for 6 months in Italy, so the allowance operates *de facto* as an employment-conditional benefit.
5. IFTC and Family Support are subject to the same means test.
6. At least 70 per cent of family income must be from earnings (or pensions).
7. There are other employment-conditional benefits in Ireland. The *part-time job incentive scheme* is open to the long-term unemployed (15 months or more) who work for less than 24 hours a week. A flat-rate payment (IR£40 per week for singles, IR£66 for one-earner couples) is paid where this is more beneficial than means-tested unemployment assistance. The *Back to Work Allowance* is paid to the long-term unemployed (1 year or more) who are aged 23 years or more and to Lone Parents (no age limit) where the person takes up self-employment or a new job (*i.e.* additional in the economy). 75 per cent of the standard means-tested unemployment or Lone-parent assistance is paid in the first year, 50 per cent in the second year and 25 per cent in the third year.

Source: United Kingdom Department of Social Security (1994), United States Department of the Treasury, United States House of Representatives (1994*b*) and information supplied by national authorities.

If earnings potential is low, more than one wage may be necessary to lift families off benefit income. But the structure of the benefit system may mean that if one member of a household is unemployed, the other may have little incentive to work. To get out of this trap, both members of a couple must find a job simultaneously. Hence, poorly-designed means-tested benefits run the risk of polarising the population into work-rich and work-poor households. In the former, at least one member of the household works and the other faces high incentives to work as well; in the latter, the incentive to work of both spouses is low.

Recent reforms in Australia have addressed this problem to some extent by giving each partner in a household where neither partner has a high level of earnings an individual benefit entitlement and reducing the METR below 100 per cent.[22] The result is that each spouse retains some incentive to work, regardless of the employment status of the partner. The balance between state and family responsibilities towards unemployed adults is politically controversial. Individualising benefits means making income support for particular individuals independent of the support they receive from other family members. Labour market priorities have led some governments to accept this. The Australian White Paper (1994, p. 187) put it thus 'The major rationale for moving towards individual entitlement is that it would encourage greater and more effective job search by both partners of a married couple. This would respond to the fact that many of the job opportunities are more likely to be gained by women than men given the increase in part-time work and the greater increase in jobs in traditionally female areas of the labour force'. A New Zealand Royal Commission suggested moving towards the individual as the basis of assessment in 1988.[23] Similar effects can be achieved by employment-conditional benefits paid to those with low incomes. Increasingly, recipients of Family Credit in the UK are not the unemployed finding low-paid jobs, but spouses in two-earner couples when his or her partner loses their job (Marsh and McKay 1993).

4.5   Employment-conditional benefits and tax credits

The distinguishing feature of employment-conditional tax credits and benefits is that they are income-tested, but payable only to those in work. These benefits are designed to shift the balance between income in and out of work, and to encourage labour force participation. By phasing out the benefit as earnings rise, resources are wholly targeted on low-paid workers. This is difficult to achieve with other policy instruments such as changing the structure of income tax or social security contributions. This phasing out, however, means higher METRs penetrate further up the earnings scale, reducing work incentives for those already in work.

4.5.1   The structure of schemes in OECD countries

Table 20 gives a brief description of the main examples of such benefits in OECD Member countries. In the United States, the value of the EITC increases as gross earnings rise, reaches a plateau at the maximum credit and is then phased out at higher earnings. Around 3.5 million families will lie in the phase-in range when the extensions of the credit envisaged in the Omnibus Budget Reconciliation Act 1993 are fully implemented. The mean marginal rate from the federal income tax and social security contributions will be minus 21.3 per cent (*i.e.* a credit). For the 2.5 m families on the plateau, the marginal rate is unchanged (averaging 17 per cent), but marginal rates for 9.8 m families in the phase-out region are increased to around 44 per cent (Holtzblatt *et al.*, 1994). As a result of the EITC, many families face higher marginal rates rather than lower. This creates an incentive for workers to reduce their hours of work. However, by increasing net income in work at all levels of earnings up to the end of the phase-out, the effect on the incentive to take a job is unambiguously positive. Canada introduced a more modest tax credit for working families with children as part of a more general reform of child support in 1993. In addition, the province of Quebec operates a more generous employment-conditional benefit: *Aide aux parents pour leurs revenus de travail*, APPORT.[24]

The Irish employment-conditional benefit, Family Income Supplement (FIS), in contrast to the US EITC, tends to be received by those in the middle of the income distribution. As a poverty-prevention measure it is less well targeted. Because of this, FIS raises METRs substantially. Its interaction with income tax and social security contributions allows METRs to exceed 100 per cent. But FIS also enhances the incentive to take a job. Replacement rates are reduced substantially (by over ten percentage points) for 8 200 families; 6 400 see a reduction of five to ten percentage points and 11 900 a smaller reduction compared with a system without this benefit (see Annex 3 for the source of these figures).

The employment-conditional benefit in the United Kingdom requires claimants to work 16 hours or more, while social assistance is restricted to those working fewer than 16 hours. The net cost of Family Credit, taking account of reduced receipt of other benefits, is two-thirds of the gross expenditure shown in Table 20. The effect of Family Credit on incentives follows the pattern in Ireland and the United States. METRs are increased for 80 per cent of the 0.5 m recipients to 70 per cent or more. Replacement rates are reduced for nearly all recipients. However, around 0.25 m two earner couples who together earn just too much to be eligible for family credit have a reduced incentive to work. If one of them were to leave their job, the family would be entitled to family credit and net family income would be little reduced. Incentives for those out of work to take a low-paid job are increased.

4.5.2   Labour-market-incentive effects

Employment-conditional credits and benefits (and indeed all benefits paid to those in work) involve a trade-off between increasing the incentive for people to take a job and encouraging those in work to reduce their hours of work. Evaluating this trade-off is an empirical question. Simulations by Scholz (1996) of the 1996 EITC suggest that the proportion of lone parents working will increase by 6.6 percentage points (see also Dickert *et al.*, 1995). A smaller 0.4 percentage point rise is predicted for married couples, since one partner in most couples works. For secondary earners, a small reduction in participation results because their additional earnings often take a family into the phase-out range, thus reducing the credit received. Scholz also estimates the reduction in hours among those working in response to the higher METR. With an assumption about the hours of those encouraged to take jobs, he estimates that the negative effect on current workers offsets around one third of the effect of increased participation so, on balance, the EITC increases aggregate hours worked. Similar results were found by Eissa and Liebman (1995) in their analysis of the 1987 expansion of the EITC.[25]

The hours rule for Family Credit in the United Kingdom was reduced from 24 to 16 hours in 1992. Dilnot and Duncan (1992) investigated the effect of the new incentive to work between 16 and 24 hours. They found that over 4 per cent of lone parents would increase their labour supply, many of whom were not working previously. Three per cent of lone-parent families would reduce hours, mainly Family Credit recipients moving from above the old ceiling to between 16 and 24 hours.

Policy reforms are often discussed on the basis of their aggregate effects. If the hours worked by those entering employment as a result of a policy reform exceed the reduction in hours worked by those already in employment, a policy reform is judged to be a good one, and vice versa. The above discussion suggests that existing employment-conditional benefits and tax credits probably would pass a criterion of success defined on this basis, but only just. However, using *aggregate* hours as a way of determining policy desirability implies that the *distribution* of hours worked would be of no interest. For both social and labour market reasons, it may be desirable to introduce reforms which promote employment of those who would otherwise be excluded from the labour market, even if the net effect is to reduce total labour supply. On this basis, it is rather clearer that such policies can be desirable.

Even so, caution is required about using such policies for two additional reasons. First, the benefits reduce the difference between the net incomes of those with low skills and those with high skills, reducing the incentive to invest in education and training. Second, a general payment to those with low earnings may lead to lower wages as a result of increased supply of low-wage labour in response to the benefit. There are two ways of viewing such an effect. One is that, although this will reduce the incentive effect on individuals, it will indirectly reduce the cost of hiring low-wage workers, potentially promoting employment (see Chapter 5 below). The other is that wages may be reduced below the value of the labour supplied, artificially boosting the profits of employers of low-wage labour. Concerns of this sort have led to suggestions that employment-conditional benefits should be combined with a minimum wage so as to prevent excessive reductions in wage rates.[26]

There are grounds for believing that employment conditional benefits have had positive effects in the countries where they already exist. Whether this means that they can be introduced in other countries with equal success is far less clear. Some examples of the effects on labour market incentives from introducing an EITC-type benefit are given in Chapter 6. To be worthwhile, the benefit must raise in-work incomes for low-wage families significantly above out-of-work incomes. But on grounds of cost and because of the effects of high METRs on work incentives, the benefit must be fully withdrawn from earnings which are received by the bulk of the working population. These constraints suggest that employment-conditional benefits will be most successful in countries where benefits are low relative to average earnings and/or the earnings' distribution is wide.

4.5.3   *Issues in scheme design*

The actual labour-market effects of employment-conditional tax credits and benefits will depend on how exactly the employment-conditional benefit or credit is designed. This section examines a number of characteristics which could condition the effectiveness of these schemes.

The impact of employment-conditional benefits depends on workers correctly perceiving the change to net income received at a particular level of earnings. In the United States, fewer than one per cent of recipients use the advance payment option enabling their employers to pay the credit through the year. The credit is therefore mainly received as a tax refund after the year end. Although this occurs in part due to ignorance of the option, in many cases people were unwilling to ask their employer for a regular payment or were concerned that they might have to re-pay the credit at the year-end if their circumstances changed (General Accounting Office, 1992). Given the marginal rate structure resulting from the credit, fluctuating income and non-cumulative withholding of income tax, the fear of over-payment is justified (Alstott, 1994, and 1995; Holt, 1992). Over half of EITC recipients also rely on professional assistance in preparing their income tax returns (Olson and

Davis, 1994). The new Independent Family Tax Credit in New Zealand will either be received fortnightly with Family Support or paid at the end of the year as a lump-sum tax credit. The link between the end-of-year credits in these schemes and work experience during the year is not likely to be clear. In contrast, payments made through the benefit system may be more transparent although take-up can be lower (Whitehouse, 1996).

If people do not claim their in-work benefit entitlement, due to stigma, costs of claiming or ignorance, then again the beneficial effect on incentives is lost. Assessment for taxation is automatic and private compared with claiming means-tested benefits. In the United States, a taxpayer will be informed by the Internal Revenue Service if they have filed a return appearing to be eligible for the EITC but have not claimed it. Empirical studies tend to show EITC take-up of over 80 per cent (Scholz, 1990 and 1994). The figures for means-tested benefits are much lower: for food stamps, the rate is 59 per cent (House of Representatives, 1993). Similarly, Family Credit and Family Income Supplement suffer from less than full take-up. The take-up rate is around 25 per cent in Ireland (Callan *et al., 1995*). In the United Kingdom it has risen from a little over 50 per cent when Family Credit was introduced in 1988 to around 80 per cent now (Department of Social Security, 1994).

Take-up of the EITC exceeds the number of families eligible. The IRS conducted a study of 1 000 EITC claimants who filed electronically in a two-week period in January. (These taxpayers may not be typical, because the majority file paper returns and the filing season extends into April.) The study found that the total credit paid out exceeded entitlements by 26 per cent. The study did not take account of IRS enforcement work or recent modifications to the EITC. If these changes are included, the rate of over-claim falls to 19 per cent. It has been suggested that the EITC is vulnerable to deception (Steuerle, 1993, Yin and Forman, 1993). The benefit means-testing process is often more rigorous than a tax audit. A problem with Family Credit is that once a claim is settled, the resulting entitlement is paid for six months regardless of fluctuations in income. The initial assessment covers earnings over a period of six weeks. This opens the scheme to deliberate manipulation of earnings to ensure eligibility, with no reassessment for six months. There is no evidence on the degree of manipulation, but estimates suggest that one half of recipients would not be eligible given their *current* income (Fry and Stark, 1993).

Tax and benefit systems operate very different sets of rules about the unit of assessment (individual or family), period of assessment (weekly, monthly, annual), the definition of income and the treatment of wealth. Using the family as the unit of assessment targets help on those with high replacement rates. Under an individual system, women married to relatively well-off men, for example, would be eligible, although they face few work disincentives from the tax and benefit system. Hence, most of these schemes are focused on families with children. In most countries, individual assessment of income tax and the fact that tax authorities do not collect information on children would preclude the use of the tax system to implement an employment-conditional payment. The definition of income for tax purposes is often less comprehensive than the one used in assessing benefits. The EITC is assessed against gross earnings and 'adjusted gross income' (taxable income), which excludes certain income sources which are exempt from income tax (such as a portion of social security and interest from municipal bonds). According to the United States General Accounting Office (1995), including all social security benefits, tax-exempt interest and non-taxable pension distributions in the measure of income used to determine EITC eligibility would save almost 6 per cent of total expenditure. But this would add significantly to the burden of administering the income tax (see also O'Neil and Nelsetuen, 1994). From 1996, taxpayers will be ineligible for the EITC if income from interest, dividends, rents and royalties exceeds $2 350, excluding around 3 per cent of EITC recipients. The US General Accounting Office (1995) concluded that operating a wealth test in the EITC would be 'impractical'. In contrast, means-tested benefit systems can successfully operate assets tests (including Family Credit in the United Kingdom and AFDC in the United States).

If gross wages are relatively sensitive to changes in taxation, wage rates will fall in response to employment-conditional benefits. The benefit will in effect act as a wage subsidy. If wages adjust fully, then net incomes in work are unchanged, and no labour supply response can be expected. Due to the shift in labour costs, a demand side response may occur, however. There is no empirical evidence of whether this is the case. Attitudinal evidence in the United Kingdom suggests that employers are insufficiently aware of the structure of Family Credit for it to have a direct effect on setting of either wages or hours of work (Callender *et al.*, 1994). There may, however, be an unconscious response to increased labour supply at low wages.

4.6   Taxation and high METRs

The benefits system can lead to disincentives for a spouse to take low-paid work if the other spouse is unemployed. Equally, the structure of social security contributions and income taxes can lead to high METRs on the earnings of spouses with an employed partner. This is particularly the case in countries where taxation is levied on couples rather than on an individual basis. Under joint taxation, a secondary earner faces the marginal rate of the primary earner from the first unit of earnings. In a progressive system, this tax rate will be higher than if the couple were taxed separately. Joint taxation provides a disincentive for secondary workers relative to independent taxation. Table 21 gives a simple breakdown of the different ways countries treat married couples in the personal income tax. Although the majority of countries have the individual as the unit of taxation, in many cases transferability of basic tax reliefs means that the tax paid by one partner is dependent on the income of the other.

Whether these disincentives for second spouses to work have actual labour market effects is difficult to prove. However, there has been a growth of part-time employment and in the numbers of secondary earners in some countries but not in others. The work disincentives in countries with family-based taxation may be an explanatory factor. Considerations of this sort explain in part the shift away from joint to individual taxation. For example, countries such as Spain and the United Kingdom moved from joint taxation during the 1980s towards individual-based systems.

The problems which the tax treatment of families can cause may be illustrated by recent Japanese experience. Until recently, a 'spouse exemption' was given to a household where the secondary earner earned less than a certain amount. Earnings beyond that amount triggered loss of all the spouse exemption, implying METRs of more than 100 per cent. As a result, part-time work of more than a minimal amount was discouraged. By allowing a tax deduction to part-time employees and gradually phasing out the spouse exemption as income rises, this disincentive has been overcome.

Table 21.   **Systems for taxing married couples**

	Basic unit	Description
Australia	Individual	no transfer of basic reliefs
Austria	Individual	no transfer of basic reliefs
Belgium	Individual	mixed system[2]
Canada	Individual	full transfer of basic reliefs[3]
Czech Republic	Individual	no transfer of basic reliefs
Denmark	Individual	full transfer of basic reliefs
Finland	Individual	no transfer of basic reliefs
France	Joint	quotient system
Germany	Joint	splitting system
Greece	Individual	no transfer of basic reliefs
Hungary	Individual	no transfer of basic reliefs
Iceland	Individual	partial transfer of basic reliefs
Ireland	Joint	married tax schedule[1]
Italy	Individual	full transfer of basic reliefs
Japan	Individual	no transfer of basic reliefs
Luxembourg	Joint	married tax schedule
Mexico	Individual	no transfer of basic reliefs
Netherlands	Individual	full transfer of basic reliefs
New Zealand	Individual	no transfer of basic reliefs
Norway	Joint	married tax schedule[1]
Portugal	Joint	quotient system
Spain	Joint	married tax schedule[1]
Sweden	Individual	no transfer of basic reliefs
Switzerland	Joint	married tax schedule
Turkey	Individual	no transfer of basic reliefs[4]
United Kingdom	Individual	no transfer of basic reliefs[5]
United States	Joint	married tax schedule[1]

Notes: Basic reliefs refers to the allowances, credits or zero-rate bands granted to all taxpayers.
1.   Couples can opt for individual taxation, but joint assessment is usually advantageous.
2.   Married couples taxed separately, but if earnings are low, then joint taxable income is calculated. Up to 30 per cent of the joint amount is assessed as the income of the lower-income spouse. If this results in a lower tax liability then the lower amount is paid.
3.   If one spouse earns below a particular limit, income is reported jointly and the member of the couple filing the return receives the credit.
4.   If each spouse earns over a particular limit and they work for different employers, they are taxed jointly.
5.   Personal allowances are assessed separately, but the additional married couples' allowance may be transferred.
Source: OECD (forthcoming), *The Tax/Benefit Position of Employees*, OECD, Paris.

4.7   Tax and benefit systems and part-time work

Unemployment benefit systems were introduced when part-time work was not a major feature of the labour market. Policy towards part-time work oscillates between competing views of the appropriate response. One view holds that it is desirable to encourage part-time work as a way of keeping benefit recipients in touch with the labour market. Many people, especially women, only wish to work part-time in the formal labour market. This suggests that paying benefits to supplement part-time earnings may be appropriate. On the other hand, the benefit system is intended to support those who cannot support themselves. By providing a sustainable alternative to full-time work or unemployment, labour supply may be reduced.

Increasingly, policies have been aimed at reducing the resulting disincentives. For example, those currently receiving the Revenu Minimum d'Insertion in France face a withdrawal rate of 50 per cent of earnings. Employers' social contributions are also reduced by 30 per cent for some categories of part-time workers. In Germany, an unemployed person (who was formerly in full-time employment) is allowed to work up to 18 hours per week with half of his pay deducted from benefits. Denmark allows a recipient of social assistance to earn up to DKr 2 000 per month for six months after three months benefit receipt. Subject to certain limits, half of all earnings of the unemployed in the United Kingdom are paid as a re-employment bonus when they find a full-time job. Ireland has a part-time job incentive scheme paid to those receiving the long-term rate of unemployment assistance who work for less than 24 hours a week. In Canada, provinces disregard some earnings (typically C\$ 50 to C\$ 200 per month, depending on family size) in the social assistance means-tests. The first \$90 per month is disregarded from Aid to Families with Dependent Children (AFDC) in the United States, with a further \$175 per month available for child-care expenses.

In many of these cases, special rules allowing part-time work to be combined with benefits are limited to those who were previously unemployed. Australia has gone further and allows those who were working full-time and whose hours have been sufficiently reduced to be entitled to means-tested benefit (although benefit entitlement remains conditional on availability for full time work if it is offered). About 15 per cent of Australian unemployment benefit recipients work part-time.

Table 22 illustrates the effects of the various disregards and special schemes that apply to part-time work. It is assumed that an unemployed person with a dependent spouse and two children works two days a week, earning two-fifths of the APW level of earnings (assumptions are thus different from those underpinning the calculations in Chapter 3).

The first year of unemployment in Ireland, in Norway when social assistance is received and in the United Kingdom when hours worked are less than 16 all follow the 'traditional' social assistance model. Apart from (small) earnings disregards, there is no immediate financial incentive to work part-time.[27] In other cases, the features of the benefit system mentioned above have an impact. Hence, the incentive to work part-time is sometimes significant, for example, in Australia. But the trade-off is apparent: the higher is the incentive to work part-time, the less attractive is full-time work compared with part-time.

The effective administration of job-search tests is important when there is an incentive to work part-time. The experiences of Belgium and Norway illustrate the problems caused by increasing the attraction of part-time relative to full-time work. Both employers and employees altered their behaviour to take advantage of the possibility of working part-time while claiming benefit. The result was 'a costly growth in the incidence of part-time work among people who would otherwise be working full-time' (OECD, 1994b). Both countries have since attempted to reduce such unintended use of the benefit system. New Zealand has recently experienced a rapid growth in part-time and seasonal employment. Administrative measures and an extension of the waiting period for re-qualification for benefits are being used to prevent inappropriate combinations of these work patterns with benefit receipt. In the United Kingdom, Family Credit is paid to those who work at least 16 hours. A supplement has recently been introduced for those working 30 hours to provide an incentive to move beyond part-time work.

One partial response to the dilemma of promoting part-time work without unnecessarily discouraging full-time work is to recognise that for some groups, such as lone parents, part-time work may be a more realistic option than full-time work. Benefit systems could be adjusted to lower benefit reduction rates for these groups, thus increasing the incentive to take part-time work, albeit at the cost of making full-time work less attractive. Similarly, METRs for the long-term unemployed on the first segment of earnings could be reduced to encourage them to maintain contact with the labour market, even where it is not possible to lift someone fully off benefit.

Table 22.   **The incentive to work part-time for an unemployed person with two children**

	Benefit	Percentage of net income in full-time work	
		Fully unemployed	Part-time worker earning 40 per cent of full-time weekly wages
Australia	Job-Search Allowance	71	86
Denmark	UI	80	88
Germany	Arbeitslosengeld (UI)	79	92
Ireland	UI/UA	65	64
	UA/Part-Time Job Incentive	70	84
Netherlands	UI	82	91
	SA with disregard	80	91
	SA without disregard	80	82
Norway	UI	73	84
	Social Assistance	83	84
Spain	UI	76	85

Note: Incomes are expressed as percentages of net incomes in full-time work at APW wages. Figures are for a couple with two children. Numbers in first column are identical to those in the first column of Table 11. An earnings disregard of 15 per cent of benefit is applied for a maximum of two years in the Netherlands. Thereafter, there is no earnings disregard.
Source: OECD Database on Taxation and Benefit Entitlements.

4.8   Tax and benefit systems and casual work

The issue of casual or temporary employment is closely related to that of part-time work, and to the problems of cash flow and uncertainty covered in Chapter 3. Many countries allow a limited amount of casual earnings without affecting benefit receipt. Table 23 shows the systems in different countries. The Table converts the value of disregarded income amounts into hours by dividing the disregard by the hourly wage rate which would result in APW income were they to work full time. In some countries, the disregard can be accumulated (Australia, Canada and Iceland). Unused disregards can be saved over time (so that A$ 30 per week equals A$ 60 after two weeks of benefit, and so on, up to a limit), be paid out upon finding employment (Iceland) or can contribute to future benefit entitlements (Canada). In general, it can be seen that disregards permit substantial amounts of part-time work only in a few cases.

Table 23. Casual employment and benefit receipt

Country	scheme	income test	disregard [1]	disregarded in hrs/w equivalents [2]	observations
Australia	UA	individual	$ 30/w of GE	1h45	if not used can be saved over time
Austria	UI	individual	Sch 3.500/m of NI	6h30	benefit ceases after disregard
Austria	UA	household	Sch 5 500/m of NI	10h10	benefit ceases after disregard
Belgium	UI	individual	-	-	accepting any job immediately destroys all benefit entitlements
Belgium	SA	household	Bfr 12 500/m of NI [3]	7h10	cannot be accumulated
Canada	UI	individual	entitlement reduced in proportion to hours worked [4]	0h	accumulation of "work credit"
Canada	SA	household	C$ 143-518/m depending on family type + 25% of remainder of NI	6h10	no accumulation of unused disregard possible
Germany	UI	individual	DM 30/w+50% of remainder of NI	2h15	no accumulation, working more than 18h/week destroys entitlements for that week
Germany	SA	household	DM 250/m of NI	2h50	no accumulation
Hungary	UI	individual	minimum wage level (HF 12 200/m)	15h30	beyond disregard benefit ceases
Hungary	SA	household	HF 1 000/m of GE	1h15	no
Iceland	UI	individual	rate related to hours worked	0h	accumulation possible, ceases after two days/week
Ireland	Ui	individual	Ir£ 10/w of net income of GE, then, stepwise reduction with earnings	1h50	no accumulation
Ireland	UA	household	Ir£ 15/day of GE individual income	2h	no accumulation, working more than three days per week destroys entitlements for that week
Luxembourg	SA	household	20% of maximum payment standard in GE	5h15	no accumulation
New Zealand	UA	individual	NZ$ 50-60/w per person depending on family type + 30-70% of remaining net income	7h40	no accumulation
Netherlands	UI/UA	individual	70% of GE for first 5h/w	0h	no, UI ceases if four days or more are spent in work
Netherlands	SA	household	local discretion		
Portugal	SA	household	80% of Esc.52000/m of GE	16h25	no
UK	UI	individual	reduced in proportion to days worked	0h	no
UK	SA	household	5-15/w of NI, depending on family	2h40	no
UK	CTB	household	£5-15/w of NI, depending on family type	2h40	no
USA	FS	household	$131-$737/m of NI depending on family type	2h50	no

Notes: W= week; M= month; h= hour.
1. Disregards can be as a percentage of gross earnings (GE) or net income (NI)
2. The equivalent in hours that can be worked before the disregard is exhausted if the beneficiary has APW full-time equivalent pay, assuming a 40 hour working week. If disregards are net of tax, the income situation of a couple with two children has been used for the conversion to hours per week.
3. Belgium: Bfr.10 000/month of gross earnings for someone without children
4. Canada: benefits are proportional to hours worked

Source: OECD Database on Taxation and Benefit Entitlements.

Casual employment may not provide a direct route into permanent work and out of benefit dependency, but it does offer the advantage of keeping people in touch with the labour market and provides a modest supplement to benefit income. Some countries have taken policy initiatives in this area recently. Australia has introduced an 'earnings-credit scheme' under which each benefit assessment period's earnings disregard can be accumulated (to a limit) and the total used to offset the impact of a temporary job on benefit entitlement. In New Zealand short-term employment has been facilitated by changes to benefit waiting periods. But the potential gains from, say, increasing the slice of earnings not subject to means tests need to be balanced against the cost of moving high withdrawal rates further up the potential earnings scale. Benefits plus the occasional addition from casual jobs may make full-time work on low pay look still less attractive. This trade off is similar to the dilemma in deciding policy towards part-time employment.

One way of encouraging casual employment that avoids this trade off is through local currency schemes. In these systems, participants trade goods and services in return for an alternative currency restricted to a given area. A centralised system is operated to keep accounts of alternative currency balances and to advertise the goods and services participants can offer. Such schemes have been expanding in a range of countries. There are around 300 each in France and the United Kingdom, 200 in Australia, 50 in New Zealand and 25 to 30 in Canada.[28] In most cases, these schemes have developed as community initiatives, although in Australia and New Zealand there has been some government assistance. Usually they have been introduced in areas with high unemployment where cash to pay for services is short. In addition to the direct labour market benefits, one of the most commonly supplied services is child minding, expanding both casual and permanent employment opportunities for those previously without access to affordable child care.

Clearly such schemes have the potential to be used for tax evasion and fraudulent benefit claims if individuals are able to shift from the primary-currency economy to working full-time in the alternative currency. In the United Kingdom, the Department of Social Security has announced that 'Local exchange trading scheme credits will not be counted as income for the purpose of the social security income test. LETS are a useful community initiative which should not be artificially discouraged by social security arrangements. ...In particular, LETS represent a form of activity that assists our clients in keeping in contact with labour market skills and habits, and indeed, with the labour market itself'. In France, transactions exceeding FF 20 000 (US$4 000) and exchanges related to the normal profession of the person (for example, a plumber exchanging plumbing services) are subject to tax. Other countries have similar regulations.

4.9 Policy responses to reduce high METRs and tackle the poverty trap

As a policy issue, high METRs have gained in importance. First, increasing numbers of people receive means-tested benefits, in part because of tighter conditions for receipt of insurance benefits. Second, social policy concerns have meant that unemployment benefits are supplemented by child benefits or family allowances. Extending these to those in work on low earnings, to avoid sharp falls in income on entering employment, have extended the range of high METRs. Third, the desire to ensure that there is a financial incentive to work has resulted in the use of employment conditional benefits.

The combined consequences of these developments were disincentives to work part-time, and for spouses of the unemployed to accept work. Recent policy reforms have looked to reduce these disincentives.

– *Earning while receiving benefits.* Countries have increased the amount which can be earned before means-tested benefits are reduced or otherwise altered the benefit system to permit a modest amount of part-time work. These disregards provide an incentive for those on social assistance to maintain a link with the labour market. Such reforms have taken place in Australia, Canada, Denmark, Ireland, the Netherlands, New Zealand and the United Kingdom. Benefits specifically for those in part-time work have been introduced in Ireland. Italy provides direct subsidies to employers and reductions in employers' social security contributions and France has recently extended its contributions exemption for part-time work. Spain reduces employer contributions for some categories of part-time work.

– *Reducing the prevalence of high METRs.* Taxes on low earnings have been reduced in several countries (Denmark, New Zealand, the United Kingdom) but budgetary constraints limit the possibilities of extending this and many other policies. Benefit reduction rates for older workers have been cut sharply in Japan. The current reform in New Zealand will lower the reduction rate from 70 to 30 per cent over a NZ$ 100 per month earnings range for lone-parent families and invalidity benefit recipients.

– *Ensuring women married to unemployed men have an incentive to work.* Australia has reduced very high METRs by individualising the benefit system. Some incentive to work is retained by the spouses of the unemployed, even where they are in receipt of means-tested benefits. A similar effect is achieved through employment conditional benefits, as in Ireland and the United Kingdom, which reduce the incentive for both spouses to leave employment when one or both becomes unemployed.

Chapter 5

TAXES, BENEFITS AND THE COST OF LABOUR

5.1   The problem

The influence of the tax and benefit system on the demand side of the labour market is as important for employment and unemployment as the supply-side incentive effects described above. Non-wage labour costs provide a disincentive to hiring workers. Employers' social security contributions are in many countries the largest of these costs.

If employer contributions are increased, then the cost of labour initially rises. However if wages fall as a result of higher contributions, in the long-term labour costs may change little: the incidence of the employer contributions falls on labour in the form of lower wages. Empirical evidence suggests that this outcome holds in the long-term in countries where wages and prices are relatively flexible. However, minimum wages, high benefit replacement rates or wage bargaining processes which favour insiders over outsiders all provide a floor to wages. Wages cannot fall below the floor, so labour costs will increase as a result of higher contributions, and the low-paid -- with wages close to legal minimum wage or current benefit levels -- will suffer higher unemployment. Since minimum wages and/or high benefit replacement rates are quite common in OECD countries, increases in social security contributions may be one source of unemployment, particularly so for low-wage unskilled labour.

Social security contributions are often structured in a proportional or regressive way, meaning that a large part of the burden falls on low-wage labour. For example, in France the contribution rate is 46 per cent of earnings just above the minimum wage. Table 24 shows that nine OECD Member countries have ceilings on contributions, which means that employers' pay a lower rate of contributions when they employ higher paid workers. In Spain, contributions are over 31 per cent of gross labour costs up to a level of around double APW earnings, with no further contributions due above that level.

The burden of contribution rates increased in eight countries over the 1980s, often by substantial amounts. Only in five countries -- Belgium, Finland, the Netherlands, Norway and Turkey -- were employer contributions significantly reduced. Australia and New Zealand do not rely on employer contributions at all (although Australia does require some employer contributions to personal retirement funds and workers compensation), and in Denmark these have never been significant.

Employers' social security contributions are only one way in which taxes affect the demand for labour. All taxes drive a wedge between the cost of labour to the firm and the return to the employee from working in terms of consumption. Table 25 shows overall tax wedges at the earnings level of the APW between 1979 and 1994. This tax wedge includes income taxes, social security contributions and consumption taxes (VAT and other general consumption taxes and excises). The overall tax wedge has been increasing in the majority of countries; only in Norway and the United States did this measure fall between 1978 and 1994. The average tax wedge rose from 45 per cent in 1978 to 49 per cent in 1985 and 50 per cent in 1990, with particularly large rises in Canada, France, Ireland and Portugal.

Table 24.   **Structure of employers' social security contributions**

	Contribution ceiling (% APW earnings)	Employers' contribution as per cent of gross earnings		
		1979	1985	1994
Austria	146	20.5	22.8	23.6
Belgium	-	24.1	25.6	34.1
Canada	105	3.0	4.9	6.6
Denmark	-	0.8	2.9	-
Finland	-	7.0	6.1	3.8
France	131	28.9	39.3	46.0
Germany	169	15.6	17.0	19.4
Greece	212	18.7	21.7	..
Iceland	-	..	2.1	2.8
Ireland	164	8.8	12.2	12.2
Italy	-	46.1	45.9	46.1
Japan	-	5.1	7.3	7.5
Luxembourg	245	15.0	15.4	15.0
Mexico	-	..	..	19.4
Netherlands	-	24.0	23.8	7.9
Norway	-	16.0	15.6	12.8
Portugal	-	19.0	20.1	24.5
Spain	219	32.6	31.2	31.6
Sweden	-	28.8	31.0	30.1
Switzerland	-	10.3	10.3	10.3
Turkey	-	10.5	9.0	7.1
United Kingdom	-	10.0	10.4	10.2
United States	229	7.6	7.1	7.7

Note: .. indicates that data are unavailable, - indicates that there is nothing to report. In Italy, there are a number of tax reliefs on employers is particular sectors and regions which imply that the illustrative rates here are not typical. National accounts data show that employers' contributions averaged 29.7 per cent of earnings in 1980, 31.9 per cent in 1985 and 36.5 per cent in 1994. Figures for Finland exclude compulsory contributions to private sector pensions (on average 15.6 per cent of earnings in 1994).
Source: OECD, *The Tax/Benefit Position of Production Workers*, various years.

A recent analysis by the European Commission (Eurostat, 1996) estimated so-called 'implicit tax rates' on labour. Personal income taxes paid on employment income and social security contributions are expressed as a percentage of total employment income from national accounts. The figures in Table 25 are the taxes paid by a hypothetical worker, whereas the implicit tax rates in Table 26 average across all taxpayers (including benefit recipients) at different earnings levels and include the effect of non-standard tax reliefs. The results show a rising tax burden on labour in nearly every EU Member state since 1980. The EU average has risen from 35 to 41 per cent over this period. This evidence confirms the picture given by the hypothetical-worker examples.

Table 25.   **Overall tax wedges 1978-1994**
Percentage of APW earnings

	1978	1985	1994
Australia	28	30	29
Belgium	57	61	61
Canada	31	37	40
Denmark	59	66	63
Finland	52	54	55
France	49	56	59
Germany	50	53	59
Iceland	-	32	36
Ireland	46	55	55
Italy	51	56	57
Japan	21	26	26
Luxembourg	48	51	52
Mexico	-	-	27
Netherlands	55	58	55
New Zealand	33	33	39
Norway	63	66	58
Portugal	36	40	47
Spain	39	43	47
Sweden	58	63	60
United Kingdom	44	48	44
United States	36	37	35

Notes: The average consumption tax rate cannot be computed for Austria, Greece, Switzerland and Turkey due to incomplete data. Data for Iceland and Mexico are unavailable for some years. The tax wedge is the difference between the cost to the employer and the consumption which can be supported from that wage. It includes employees' and employers' social security contributions, personal income taxes and consumption taxes, see OECD (1995*a*). The average rate of consumption tax is calculated from national accounts data. Non-standard income tax reliefs (such as those for mortgage payments) are not taken into account. Non-wage labour costs other than social security contributions, are ignored. The figures for Norway exclude the effects of taxes on oil. Taxes are as defined in OECD *Revenue Statistics* (OECD, 1996*b*). They do not take account of social security benefits that may be received conditional on having made contributions.
Source: OECD, *The Tax/Benefit Position of Production Workers*: 1995 *Edition* and OECD National Accounts.

        The problem caused by a large and growing tax wedge has been recognised in many countries (Belgium, France, Germany, Ireland, Italy and the Netherlands), but putting reform into practice has proved difficult. General cuts in social security contribution rates are extremely expensive. As a consequence, many countries have attempted to target rate reductions on groups with particular labour market problems, such as the long-term unemployed, those in apprentice schemes, in disadvantaged regions, or the young. Of course, some of the people benefiting would have been hired even without the contribution reduction (the dead-weight cost), and new employees may displace existing employees. A number of studies of OECD countries have suggested that programmes of wage subsidies or cuts in social contributions have therefore not been 'self-financing' (see Gautié *et al.,* 1994, a conclusion recently reaffirmed by the Belgian Bureau Fédéral du Plan, 1995). Savings from reduced benefits payments plus increased taxes as the demand for labour grows is lower than the cost of reductions in contributions. Many countries have implemented these schemes at one time or another and they are reviewed in OECD (1993c). Nevertheless, targeting cuts in employers contributions on particular groups (such as the low paid, youths or the long-term unemployed) may be justified if long-term gains from providing work experience for targeted groups outweigh these short-term costs. In some circumstances, cuts in social security contributions are analogous to temporary wage subsidies paid to employers to hire labour.

Table 26.   **Implicit tax rates on labour, 1980-1993**

Per cent	1980	1985	1993
Austria	37.9	40.9	42.3
Belgium	38.4	44.8	44.9
Denmark	38.1	39.5	41.2
Finland	-	-	54.7
France	37.1	40.4	43.9
Germany	36.4	39.5	41.2
Greece	-	-	40.4
Ireland	23.4	30.2	31.2
Italy	31.9	36.6	43.2
Luxembourg	33.6	33.3	31.2
Portugal	-	25.2	34.7
Netherlands	45.6	50.9	52.5
Spain	28.8	32.0	36.9
Sweden	50.9	52.7	52.1
United Kingdom	24.8	26.1	24.9

Notes: Data for Spain are 1992 rather than 1993. Data for Portugal are for 1986 and 1991.
A - indicates that data are unavailable.
Source: Eurostat 1996.

If other taxes are increased to recoup the revenue from cuts in social security contributions, negative labour market consequences of these tax hikes must also be considered. Cutting one part of the wedge while increasing another (employees' contributions or consumption taxes) does not shift the overall tax burden away from labour. Such a reform *might* have beneficial employment effects, but only under a number of restrictive conditions: *if* a reduction in employers' charges does not lead to higher wages, and *if* increases in other taxes do not result in higher wage claims by employees, there might be some positive effect on employment. The fundamental point is that the tax burden must not just be *shifted* from one form of labour tax to another but that the tax burden on labour must be *cut* (see OECD, 1995a).

One way to cut the tax burden on labour is to spread the burden of financing social protection more widely than is currently the case. An extension of the contributions base to cover other sources of income as well as wages would potentially reduce the tax burden on labour. However, as described in the *Jobs Study*, earnings account for nearly 60 per cent of household incomes on average (although it is rather lower in Belgium and Italy and higher in the United States and Canada). This limits the extent to which taxes can be shifted to unearned income sources, such as capital and transfers. Even then the implicit cut in the replacement rate of benefits (including pensions) may be difficult to maintain without compensatory increases in benefit levels.

If the social-contributions base is deemed appropriate, but the contribution rate is high enough to have a detrimental effect on the labour market, the only way of reducing contribution rates is to cut the benefits which they finance. But this might also be unacceptable. Benefits may be generous as a result of a social consensus that inequality should be reduced or to enable people to avoid having to take a low-wage, dead-end job.

Such a reassessment is made more difficult by the structure of social contributions in many countries. Employers often have a far higher contributions' rate than do employees. This can lead to the illusion that the employer bears the largest burden in financing social benefits. In fact, although the employer may be responsible for withholding contributions, in the longer run it is workers who ultimately pay for the benefits, either through reduced real wages or reduced employment. Shifting the cost of providing social security from employer to employee contributions may have little direct economic effect in the long-term, but by increasing the transparency of the system, it will promote more rational decisions about social spending. A shift from employers' to employees' contributions while at the same time increasing pre-tax wages so that labour costs and net earnings remain unchanged may have long-run benefits if as a result debate on the benefit system gets more informed. This seems to have been the result of a reform of this nature in the Netherlands in 1990.

5.2   Policy responses to reduce the cost of hiring low-wage workers

European Union Member states have committed themselves to reduce non-wage labour costs by an average of one to two percentage points of GDP, as advocated in European Commission (1993). Recent reforms in these and other countries include:

− *Reducing employers' charges.* Finland, Portugal and Spain have cut social security contributions, by 1.5, 0.75 and one percentage point respectively. Reductions in employer contributions in Luxembourg are worth around 0.5 per cent of GDP. In other countries, the cuts have been focused on the low-paid. The United Kingdom has cut employer contributions by one percentage point for the lowest paid 20 per cent of the workforce, with a 0.2 percentage point cut in the main rate. In Ireland, employers' contributions on low earnings have been cut from 12.2 to 9 per cent. In Belgium, a large reduction in employer contributions (0.7 per cent of GDP) was focused on the low-paid. In France there is an exemption until 1998 from family and health contributions for all those earning under 160 per cent of the minimum wage. The Netherlands quite substantially reduced the wage tax remittance from employers for low-paid employees in 1996, replacing other targeted measures introduced in 1995.

− *Broadening the contributions' base.* France has increased the use of the *Contribution Sociale Généralisée,* which is levied not only on labour income but on a wide range of other sources of income. Portugal has shifted some elements of the financing of the social protection system away from employers' charges towards VAT.

− *Reducing social contributions for certain groups.* Targeted reductions in social security contributions are used widely. Recent reforms in this area include measures focused on youths and first-time workers in Belgium, Ireland, Portugal and Spain, on the long-term unemployed in Portugal and the United Kingdom, on particular regions in Greece and Spain, on small- and medium-sized enterprises in France and on part-time work in Italy.

Chapter 6

TRADE-OFFS IN TAX AND BENEFIT REFORMS

Most policy reforms in the field of taxes and benefits involve trade-offs, between financial and social costs, between replacement rates and METRs, and between reductions in METRs for some and higher METRs for others. Microsimulation models can illustrate these trade-offs. They show the budgetary cost or yield of a reform, indicate who are the gainers and losers and the numbers of those for whom work incentives are improved and the number who see their incentives worsen. These changes in incentives may cause changes in behaviour. If, for example, a reform was very successful at moving people from unemployment into jobs, the 'second-round' effect would include lower public spending on benefit payments to the unemployed and higher taxes collected on earnings. The budgetary cost would be lower than the one found when behavioural changes are ignored (the 'first-round' effect). It would be extremely useful if reliable estimates of these second-round effects could be obtained. Unfortunately, the complexity and uncertainty of estimates makes it very difficult to simulate behavioural effects of tax and benefit reform. In particular, estimates of increased participation in employment are extremely unreliable. Furthermore, microsimulation models cannot easily reflect problems in take-up of benefits, although present take-up rates may be assumed indicative of behavioural responses to be expected. Predictions based on legal entitlement certainly abstract from real-world issues such as lack of information and compliance costs.

Microsimulation models can therefore only give a partial picture of the effects and potential of a particular reform option. But they can still be revealing. If, for example, the number of people who experience an increase in labour market incentives (reduced replacement rates or METRs) is far larger than the number of people who face reductions in incentives, the labour market effects of the reform can confidently be expected to be positive. The extent to which improved incentives translate into more jobs of course depends on labour demand conditions, as well as the change in labour supply. The social effects of the policy change can be assessed by looking at the distributional effects of the change, and the first-round revenue cost of a change gives some idea of the cost-effectiveness of the change.

A reform which is effective in 'making work pay' in one country may not be appropriate in another because the pattern of changes in working incentives differs. This chapter assesses five broad reform options using the microsimulation models described in annex 3, with the aim of identifying whether differences between countries do affect the relative effectiveness of these policy options. The results must be interpreted in the light of the limitations of microsimulation modelling. Furthermore, the following reforms are not revenue neutral; the potential positive or negative effects on incentives, and social objectives of how the reforms are to be financed or how the revenues saved will be spent will determine the overall effects of any reform.

6.1   Simulation 1: Reducing unemployment benefits by one fifth

6.1.1   *Effects on labour market incentives*

In Germany, this policy would reduce replacement rates for half the employed population by five to ten percentage points, with most of the rest facing a fall of one to five percentage points. A similar pattern is found in Ireland, New Zealand and the United Kingdom. In these countries the largest falls in replacement rates are found among those who started with high replacement rates. Here the reform is effective in ameliorating the most severe unemployment traps. METRs are also reduced for a proportion of the population, improving work incentives, because the reduction in means-tested benefits means that they are clawed back completely at lower income levels.

6.1.2   *Distributional and revenue effects*

The reduction in net replacement rates and the budgetary savings from a 20 per cent cut in unemployment benefits are often smaller than might be expected. This is because of the effects of taxation and of other benefits related to net income. In Canada, for example, the cost of unemployment benefits would fall by C$ 2.8 bn (US$2.2 bn at purchasing power parity exchange rates, OECD, 1995*h*), but increased child support payments and reduced tax receipts reduce the net gain to the public budget to C$ 1.8 bn (US$1.4 bn).

The financial costs of this policy are concentrated on those with lowest initial incomes: 2.7 million out of the 4.3 million poorest German households would on average lose more than 2 per cent of household income, with the average loss of those affected in the bottom quintile being around DM 170 (US$81) per month. Far fewer are affected in the highest decile (around 650 000 households), but their average monthly loss of income is higher -- DM 220 (US$105) -- reflecting the earnings-related nature of the German benefit system. In the more highly means-tested systems of Canada, Ireland, New Zealand and the United Kingdom, the losses are even more concentrated in the lower income quintiles.

6.1.3   *Assessment*

As might be expected, the sharp cut in benefit generosity has a substantial effect on labour market incentives, and would lead to budgetary savings. The distributional effects are the main argument against this kind of reform. The more flat-rate benefits are used, the more a benefit cut increases incentives for the group that finds work least financially rewarding, but the starker will be the distributional consequences.[29]

6.2   Simulation 2: Reducing benefit reduction rates by 20 percentage points

6.2.1   *Effects on labour market incentives*

High METRs can be lowered by cutting the benefit reduction rate (BRR), but only at the cost of extending the benefit system upwards into the income distribution. Table 27 shows the change in METRs as a result of a large reduction in the BRR. More than three times as many people face higher METRs as a result of the reform than face lower METRs (compare columns 5 to 7 with columns 1 to 3). However, those who do face lower METRs are predominantly those who had high

METRs before. In column 1 where falls in METRs are largest, nearly all individuals previously had METRs of 80 to 100 per cent. In contrast, the big increases in METRs (column 7) are experienced by those who had relatively low METRs (40 to 80 per cent) before the reform.

Table 27. **Change in METRs in Germany as a result of a 20 percentage point reduction in withdrawal rates for social assistance and housing benefits**
(thousands of individuals initially affected)

Pre-reform METR	Change in marginal effective tax rates (% points)							
	1	2	3	4	5	6	7	8
	-10 or less	-10 to -5	-5 to -1	-1 to 1	1 to 5	5 to 10	10 or more	total
less than 20	0	0	0	4 133	0	0	6	4 139
20-40	0	0	3	2 918	10	5	140	3 076
40-60	0	9	2	6 693	15	43	1 511	8 273
60-80	2	2	57	3 867	51	74	866	4 919
80-100	774	31	19	193	19	3	56	1 095
Total	776	42	81	17 804	95	125	2 579	21 502

Source: see annex 3.

In the United Kingdom there would also be a trade-off: reductions in METRs for 850 000 households would be offset by increases for 650 000 housholds who would become eligible for a means-tested benefit to which they were not previously entitled.

Similar results are observed in reform simulations for the United States. Reductions in the withdrawal rate applied to Aid for Families with Dependent Children would reduce METRs by at least 10 per cent for 80 000 households. A further 50 000 households benefit from some reduction: lone-parent families in particular would face lower METRs. But nearly 200 000 households would face increases in their METRs of 10 per cent or more. As in Germany, the falls in METRs would be concentrated on those with initially high METRs whereas those with low METRs (*i.e.* those who were previously not eligible for the benefit but who become so) would encounter METR increases.

Sometimes, however, it is possible to be rather clearer about the desirability of alterations to METRs. Family Income Supplement in Ireland is currently withdrawn against gross income. Rebasing the entitlements to be calculated on *net* income would cost IR£ 38 m (US$58 m). 22 200 individuals would see large drops in METRs (all 19 800 Irish workers who currently face METRs of more than 100 per cent would see their METRs fall substantially). 33 000 workers would become eligible for the benefit and would as a result face increases in their METRs; their pre-reform METRs were in the 20 to 60 per cent range. Average effective tax rates would also generally fall, reflecting higher in-work incomes. However, even in this case some caution is required. The above figures assume full take-up of FIS. As discussed above, the Irish experience is that take-up of FIS is low.

6.2.2   *Distributional and revenue effects*

A 20 percentage-point cut in benefit reduction rates for social assistance and housing benefits in Germany would cost DM 12 bn (US$5.7 bn). A similar reform of all means-tested

73

programmes in the United Kingdom (including Family Credit) would require £860 m (US$1.35 bn). However, this assumes no behavioural effects from the reform. Increase in work effort from those facing lower METRs might reduce the budgetary cost; against this, those with higher METRs might reduce their labour supply and increase their benefit receipt. Financial gains would be concentrated in the bottom three income quintiles (those with very low incomes tend not to be working at present, so they would not gain immediately unless they found a job). A third of lone-parent families would gain from the reform, as would one-fifth of couples with children. Similarly, in the United States and the United Kingdom, those most likely to gain financially from such a reform would be middle-income families rather than the very poorest who have no earnings (at least before the incentive to earn was strengthened).

6.2.3   Assessment

The reform of benefit withdrawal rates seems more clearly beneficial in the case of Ireland than it is in Germany, the United Kingdom or the United States because the ratio of reductions in METRs to increases is far more favourable. This in turn reflects the distribution of earnings in the area over which METRs are being changed. In Germany, the extension of social assistance takes the benefit system into a dense part of the earnings distribution. This would also happen in the United States. The labour market effects of such a change might still be considered to be positive if very high METRs are thought to have serious disincentive effects. Nevertheless, the labour market effects of some reduction in BRRs might be considered positive if high METRs have serious disincentive effects for a socially disadvantaged group (like most recipients of AFDC in the United States and of Sozialhilfe in Germany). Drawing this group into part-time work is now a policy priority in many countries, and this may well outweigh the economic cost of potentially reduced hours of work by some middle-income groups in employment.

6.3   Simulation 3: The effects of employment-conditional tax credits and benefits

6.3.1   Effects on labour market incentives

The above review of the effects of already existing employment-conditional tax credits or benefits suggested that they had, on balance, a positive effect overall on labour supply. To see whether this could be replicated in other countries, a scheme approximating the US EITC was modelled, giving a credit of 25 per cent of gross earnings up to one third of median earnings. A plateau between one third and half of APW is followed by a phase-out at 20 per cent of gross earnings. For those currently in employment in Germany, 29 per cent of those affected would be in the 'phase-in' region (METRs fall), 21 per cent in the plateau region (METRs unchanged) and 50 per cent in the phase-out region (METRs increased). The incentive effects are likely to reduce overall labour supply of those with jobs before the reform. If those without jobs were to find work at a low wage (the earnings of the lowest decile), replacement rates would fall significantly for 234 000 workers. These non-employed people would face a significant incentive to find employment. But over 200 000 people without jobs would face reduced incentives to enter employment; their spouses would qualify for the benefit if they did not work, but not if they did. The higher the wage assumed for those entering employment, the more this disincentive effect dominates over the incentive effect.

Existing employment-conditional benefits are mainly or exclusively aimed at families with children. Extending Family Credit to single people in the United Kingdom would increase METRs for new recipients but replacement rates would mainly fall, with part-time work becoming more attractive. Hence, the extension would almost certainly expand employment but at substantial budgetary cost. The EITC is paid at a low rate to single people in the United States. Were it to be paid at the same rate as is paid to families with children, marginal tax rates would fall for 1.7 million households and would rise for 5.5m. Again, the increases would be much smaller than the decreases. Replacement rates for the currently employed would fall by five to ten percentage points for 0.8 m households, and by one to five percentage points for 2.8 m households. They would increase for 2.3 m households. If expected earnings for the currently unemployed are low, there would be large positive effects on the incentive to work.

6.3.2   *Distributional and revenue effects*

The cost of the assumed tax-credit scheme in Germany would be DM 12 bn (US$5.7 bn). Because the earnings distribution is narrower in Germany, proportionally many more families would be eligible. So the cost would be higher than in the United States, if the credit had a broadly similar structure relative to median earnings.

Extending Family Credit in the United Kingdom to childless people would have a gross cost of £2 bn (US$3.1 bn), doubling current spending, with 1.7 million new claimants. Spending on other benefits would fall by £0.25 bn (US$0.4 bn). Those in the bottom income quintile would be the main gainers.

6.3.3   *Assessment*

The labour market effects of employment-conditional benefits involve a trade-off. Existing schemes in Ireland, the United Kingdom and the United States probably have positive effects on *overall* labour supply: the extra hours worked by people drawn into employment outweigh reductions in hours worked by people facing higher METRs. But expansion of the schemes to cover households without children is very expensive, and seem unlikely to have as large effects.

Grafting a scheme very close to the United States EITC onto the German labour market would not be sensible. The narrower earnings distribution in Germany brings many more people into the credit (making it very expensive) and most of them are in the phase-out range with high METRs. A similar conclusion was reached in an analysis of the potential effect of such schemes in Denmark (Ministry of Finance, 1995). Although the incentive for the unemployed to take a job would be improved, the negative impact on those in jobs would be more serious than in the United States. Either a higher phase-out or a lower level of maximum credit may improve the trade-off. Employment conditional benefits may have a role beyond the countries which already have them, but they should not be seen as a panacea.

6.4   Simulation 4: Family or individual taxation?

6.4.1   *Effects on labour market incentives*

Family-based taxation systems, which continue to be used in a few OECD countries, provide a disincentive for secondary earners to enter the labour marker, particularly at low wages, compared with individual-based tax systems. Individual taxation can be implemented in many ways with substantially different labour market effects. In this simulation, the current tax treatment of

75

single persons was applied to all members of a household. To ensure revenue neutrality, a new individual exemption of $4 000 compared with $2 050 in the United States 1990 tax system was modelled. The reform would be very effective at reducing the highest marginal rates: 86 per cent of the one-and-a-half million people with METRs of more than 40 per cent would see their marginal rates fall, with none seeing increases. But around a third of those with the lowest marginal rates (under 20 per cent) would see an increase in their marginal rate of over five percentage points.

Germany also currently taxes couples on their total income. A reform made revenue-neutral by increasing child benefits would increase METRs for more than ten times as many individuals in employment as those who would see reductions in METRs. Replacement rates would increase for twice as many workers (although usually only by a very small amount) as would experience a decrease. However, the incentives facing those without jobs would increase substantially. In particular, the non-employed (often the non-working spouse of a worker) would face large increases in the incentive to work.

6.4.2   *Distributional and revenue effects*

In the United States, around 16 m couples would lose an average of around $500 from moving to fully individual taxation, with 16 m single individuals and 2 m couples gaining. The German reform would redistribute resources from couples with no children to couples with children and (especially) lone-parent families. All income quintiles except the top would gain on average from the reform.

6.4.3   *Assessment*

The move to individual taxation could raise large amounts of revenue if everyone were accorded the same tax treatment as already applies to single people. The way in which this revenue is spent proves to have a large impact on the overall effects of the reform package. In the German case considered, families with children gain. In the United States case, single people and individuals in the low to middle income range see their position improve. In each case, the reform is very effective in increasing the incentive for the non-employed to enter employment, in particular spouses of working partners. But marginal tax rates for those already working would go up.

6.5   Simulation 5: Restructuring social security contributions

6.5.1   *Effects*

The modelled reform is designed to show the effect of a revenue-neutral restructuring of social security contributions. The reform aims to reduce the burden on the low-paid by introducing a floor to the system where earnings below the floor are exempt from contributions. As no changes are made to benefit entitlements, this implies a change in any current link between contributions and benefits. This change is financed, first, by eliminating any ceilings to contributions and, second, by an increase in the contribution rate. This reform differs from the others in that the labour market and distributional effects coincide. A reduction in the taxes paid on low earnings is intended to reduce the overall cost of labour or increase the net incomes (and hence the incentive to work) of those with that level of earnings.

In the United States, the floor was set at $9 275 -- one third of median earnings. The $51 300 ceiling for contributions was eliminated and an increase in the contribution rate from 7.65 to 11.5 per cent of gross earnings on both employer and employee was also necessary to achieve revenue neutrality. This reform would be highly progressive: the break-even point is around $28 000, with those earning less gaining and those earning more losing. As a result, the bottom 80 per cent of the income distribution would gain an average of $350 with the top 20 per cent losing $1 700. A similar reform in Germany which exempted the first DM 1 450 (US$690) per month from social security contributions would, if no revenue compensating reforms were undertaken, benefit higher income groups more than those with lower incomes. Over 1.7 million households would see falls in METRs as they would no longer have to pay social security contributions.

6.5.2   Assessment

The reform would achieve its aim of increasing the incentive to hire low-paid workers. Replacement rates in the United States would fall for around 53 per cent of the employed. All replacement rates over 80 per cent are reduced, as are nearly all between 40 and 60 per cent. The 18 per cent of employees with increased replacement rates all lie within the group with the lowest replacement rates (less than 40 per cent). There are two main obstacles to this reform. It may not be desirable to increase taxes on higher earnings. Although it makes sense in countries where the link between the value of social security contributions and benefits received is relatively weak, it will not work in countries where the social security system has a strong actuarial link.

6.6   Evaluating policy trade-offs

Stability in tax and benefit systems is desirable. Along with co-operation and co-ordination between different agencies involved in collecting taxes and paying benefits, stability increases system transparency. Reforms can disrupt reasonable expectations of benefits, particularly when benefit entitlements are linked to past social security contributions. Transitional reliefs designed to protect existing beneficiaries can be extremely complex. But the desire for a stable system, administrative inertia and a fear of to electorally estrange losers from reforms should not be allowed to prevent desirable change.

The microsimulation analyses presented above show how patterns of incentives can be changed. But behavioural responses are difficult to predict and may be unexpected. Piloting change in experiments, limited to certain areas or groups, allows governments to try out a broader range of policy options while avoiding over-frequent changes in tax liabilities and benefit entitlements for the majority.

- In some countries, regional governments have been given the freedom to search for better alternatives to the status quo. In Canada, provincial governments have experimented with changes in benefit reduction rates. In the United States, 37 states have changed AFDC rules, with 9.9 million recipients now required to work, take more responsibility for their children, or sign personal responsibility contracts (see Office of Management and Budget, 1996).

- Numerous experiments have been carried out in the United States. In the Seattle and Denver Income Maintenance Experiments (SIME/DIME) in the 1970s, around 5 000 families in each city were assigned to one of two groups. The first faced a negative income tax (*i.e.* one which pays a credit to those with the lowest incomes). The second was a control group, who continued to face the existing tax and welfare system. Different negative income tax regimes, with varying guaranteed minimum incomes and reduction rates were tried. Work histories of people in these experiments were collected over a period of up to three years. Studies of these data produced useful conclusions on individuals' responses to changes in incentives (see Keeley and Robins, 1980, Robins and West, 1980 and 1983, and Johnson and Pencavel, 1982 and 1984). Other experiments within the tax and benefit system which have current policy relevance include those for 'back-to-work' bonuses referred to above (O'Leary *et al*, 1995, and Meyer, 1995).

- In the United Kingdom, four schemes have been or are being piloted: *Workstart* (a subsidy to employers who recruit people who have been unemployed for more than two years), *Jobmatch* (a six-month duration allowance to the long-term unemployed taking part-time employment) and *Earnings Top-Up* (an extension of in-work benefits to single people and couples without children). In the case of Earnings Top-Up, two alternative schemes will be implemented covering 20 000 people in eight areas paying an average supplement of £18 to single people and £25 to married couples. Information on a control group for which the benefits system is unchanged will provide a benchmark for measuring the effects of the measure (see Department of Social Security, 1995*b*). The *Parents Plus* scheme is directed at lone parents who under current rules are not required to seek work to receive benefits. The scheme will be piloted in 12 areas. In four areas, private sector tenders will be invited, with payment on results (*i.e.* the numbers moving into work, training schemes, education *etc.*). Participation is voluntary, and involves case workers assessing barriers to lone-parents' employment and how they may be overcome including assistance with job search and with child-care costs. Again, random assignment to treatment and control groups will allow a detailed and accurate assessment of the effectiveness of the programme.

- In France, a scheme making compensatory payments to the unemployed who take low-paid jobs was introduced as an experiment limited to 10 000 participants in 1993.

- In Canada, the 'self-sufficiency project' is an experimental employment-conditional benefit piloted in New Brunswick and British Columbia. For those working 30 hours a week or more, it pays half the difference between actual earnings and a reference level of earnings (from C$ 30 000 to C$ 37 000). The benefit reduction rate is 50 per cent. Early evidence (Lui-Gurr *et al., 19*94) suggests that the experimental scheme did result in more people leaving social assistance than was the case in a control group.

Chapter 7

CONCLUSIONS

If work does not pay, people will be reluctant to work. For the majority of the population in the OECD area, there are clear, immediate, financial incentives to work. But such incentives may be lacking for many people with low potential wages, particularly if they have children. Some will work in spite of this, because work experience improves long-run job prospects or for other reasons. Nevertheless, for these groups, social and labour market goals may clash. Benefits need to be high enough to ensure income is adequate, but this may mean that taking a job brings little or no extra income, trapping families in a cycle of dependency.

Three problems caused by tax and benefit systems are considered in this Report. The first is the "unemployment trap" which occurs when benefits are high compared with expected incomes when working. The second problem is the 'poverty trap': low-wage workers have little immediate financial incentive to increase their hours worked. Furthermore, the incentive to work part-time or to invest in education and training to move up the wage ladder is blunted. The third is the problem of high taxes on labour leading to a reduction in the demand for labour, particularly for low-skilled labour.

There are no easy or obvious solutions to these problems. Cutting benefits is the simplest way of increasing the incentive to work, but it is not necessarily the best and the social costs may be unacceptable. If benefits are reduced to an inadequate level or if job-search is inefficiently short, poverty may increase and welfare be diminished. Few countries have opted for more than marginal cuts in benefits. Nevertheless, if benefits are higher than potential in-work incomes, long-term benefit dependency out of work may be encouraged. The benefit level may need to be cut. In addition, the duration of earnings-related benefits should be designed to encourage reappraisal of acceptable wages by those who do not rapidly find work.

Another potential solution which has attracted much interest in recent years, is employment-conditional tax credits or benefits. These can reduce the unemployment trap by increasing in-work incomes for the low-paid at lower budgetary cost than general tax cuts. But such policies are not appropriate everywhere. The wider is the earnings' distribution and the lower are METRs before introducing the benefit, the greater is the likelihood that employment-conditional benefits will increase aggregate labour supply. These schemes are best limited to families with children because they usually have higher benefit entitlements and therefore smaller work incentives.

Two areas where balancing the various objectives of tax and benefit systems is particularly difficult are the benefit position of spouses of unemployed persons and the combination of part-time work with benefit receipt. The number of recipients of means-tested benefits has increased rapidly in nearly every OECD country because of failure to qualify for, and exhaustion of, insurance benefits, growth in youth unemployment and in the number of lone-parent families. Depending on the design of the means-test, it can reduce the incentive to work part-time or for low earnings not just by the unemployed person but also by their spouse. Means-tested benefits should be designed so that each member of the household has an incentive to work, *e.g.* by separating benefit entitlements for individuals. Part-time work which promotes contact with the labour market should be encouraged for those such categories as lone-parent families or the long-term unemployed for whom full-time work may not be a realistic option. Allowing part-time work to be combined with reduced benefit receipt for a limited period will help such groups. But experience suggests that it is important to maintain tight controls on part-time unemployment benefits to guard against abuses.

Through tax and benefit systems governments are pursuing multiple objectives, including, *inter alia,* raising revenue; insuring against labour-market risk; supporting families without resources; and trying to preserve incentives to work. It is inevitable that not all of these goals can be achieved simultaneously. But this report has identified avoidable barriers to employment caused by administrative complexities, poor integration of the various parts of the tax and benefit systems and badly designed means-tests. It has also indicated several policy areas where well-designed policies will increase employment opportunities for the most disadvantaged, but (slightly) reduce work incentives for the majority. The social and labour market consequences of permanently excluding a significant minority of the population from the world of work are apparent in too many OECD countries for such policies to be spurned.

Annex 1

MEASURING INCENTIVES

For somebody in work, a high replacement rate is desirable. It implies that the fall in income following job loss would be small. From the point of view of someone without a job, high replacement rates are undesirable. They imply that after taking into account the loss of benefit on entering employment, there would be very little change in household income. The term 'replacement rate' is being used in two senses; one relates to income replaced following job-loss, the other refers to the implicit tax on working caused by loss of benefits. In most cases, use of the single term replacement rate to cover both concepts is not confusing. But occasionally a different way of calculating the replacement rate is required according to the precise use to which the relationship between incomes in and out of work is being put.

The differences between the way in which the two concepts might lead to different replacement rates are illustrated in the Table below. (The Table abstracts from the effects of taxation for the sake of simplicity.) In the first line, it is assumed that a single person receives 80 when unemployed and 100 when employed. The loss of income if someone employed lost their job would be 20, and the replacement rate relevant to this concept would be 80/100 = 80 per cent. The implicit tax rate on working caused by the loss of benefit would be one minus the change in income divided by the increase in earnings, 1 - 20/100 = 80 per cent. The two different concepts imply the same replacement rate. In the second line, however, it is assumed that someone in exactly the same circumstances has capital income. Incomes in and out of work are then higher, so the replacement rate in the sense of ratios of incomes is higher than 80. But the replacement rate in the sense of the implicit tax remains at 80.

In the third line, the position of a single earner in a couple is considered. Assuming the spouse has no income, the position is identical to that of the single person. But this is not so where there are two earners. The fourth line assumes considers the replacement rate which might be calculated were there two people earning 100 each, but the second earner has no individual benefit entitlement. Were the second earner to be without a job, the income of the family would be the earnings of the first earner -- 100. The replacement rate compared with when the second earner works is therefore 100/200. But the replacement rate in the sense of the implicit tax would be zero -- no benefits would be lost were the individual to enter employment.

When there is no capital income and where there is only one earner in the household, the replacement rate under either concept is identical. Figure 2, Table 2 and the replacement rate tables are calculated for hypothetical households, abstract from capital income and only cover one-earner households. The replacement rates can be interpreted either as being ratios of family income or implicit taxation. But when real data is used, as in all the chapters discussing microsimulation models, the choice of which way of calculating the replacement rate matters. If simple ratios of family income are used, then in all countries a minority of households have very high replacement rates because of the effects of capital income. In countries with large numbers of two-earner households, replacement rates for a much greater number of individuals are apparently very high. Both these causes of high replacement rates imply little incentive to work, but in each case this is not because of the effects of the tax and benefit system, but because each earner only provides a proportion of family income. In this study, which is concerned not about explaining participation rates *per se* but rather the effects of tax and benefit systems on incentives to work, the second measure of replacement rates, which abstracts away from the effects of income sources other than the earnings and benefits of the person in question, is preferable. This is sometimes called an individualised replacement rate, or an average effective tax rate.

Table A1   **Measuring incentives**

	Benefits when unemployed	Earnings when employed	Capital income	Ratio of family income	Average effective tax rate
Single person	80	100	0	80%	80%
Single person	80	100	10	82%	80%
First earner	80	100	0	80%	80%
Second earner	0	100	0	50%	0%

Source: OECD.

The income concept when calculating replacement rates can vary for other reasons:

– **Gross and net replacement rates**. Net replacement rates take account of the effects of taxation and social security contributions; gross replacement rates and the OECD index do not (see Table 5).

– **Benefit coverage**. The OECD index does not include any benefits relating to children, housing or low incomes. Tables 7 and 9 show the impact of including them. Where indicated, social assistance is included in the same way (Table 10).

– **Employers and employees taxes**. The replacement rates take no account of taxes paid by employers. This is consistent with the assumption that employers' social security contributions have no effect on wages. This implies that a shift in taxation from the employee to the employer might increase work incentives. In fact, for reasons discussed in Chapter 5, they probably would not increase. The individualised replacement rates calculated using the microsimulation models are derived taking account of employers' social contributions. This is consistent with the assumption that the full burden of such taxes falls on wages.

Annex 2

REPLACEMENT RATE CALCULATIONS

The replacement rates presented in Chapter 3 are only a selection of all rates which can be calculated using different assumptions. To consider how the replacement rates are related to one another, consider the table below, which shows some intermediate steps in the calculation of the net replacement rates for Germany.

Table A2. **Replacement rate calculations for Germany**

	Incomes out of work			Incomes in work			Replacement rates (Incomes out of work/incomes in work)		
	Single	Couple	Couple, 2 children	Single	Couple	Couple, 2 children	Single	Couple	Couple 2 children
Gross income	19822	22302	26115	53512	53512	53512	37	42	49
tax	*0*	*0*	*0*	*20475*	*16342*	*14535*			
After tax income	19822	22302	26115	33037	37170	38977	60	60	67
family benefits	*0*	*0*	*3180*	*0*	*0*	*2400*			
After family benefits income	19822	22302	29295	33037	37170	41377	60	60	71
housing benefits	*179*	*1459*	*2852*	*0*	*0*	*0*			
After housing benefits	20001	23761	32146	33037	37170	41377	61	64	78

Source: OECD Database on Taxation and Benefit Entitlements.

If a worker has gross earnings of DM 53 512 per year, then the unemployment insurance benefits to which he or she will be entitled if they were to lose that job vary for the three types of household. Hence the replacement rates calculated on the basis of gross incomes in and out of work are 37, 42 and 49 per cent. The difference between the first and the second line in Table 2 reflects only differences in gross unemployment benefit payments.

No tax is paid on unemployment benefit, so after-tax incomes out of work in Germany are the same as pre-tax incomes. However, tax will be paid on DM 53 512 of earnings. The amount of tax varies according to family circumstances; hence net after-tax incomes for the three types of household diverge. The differences between adjacent columns in Table 5 reflect the effects of deducting tax and social security contributions from earnings in work and also benefits received when out of work.

Family benefits are paid to families with children both in and out of work in Germany, as in most other countries. In many countries, the amount of benefit is the same regardless of income, but this is not so in Germany where such benefits are partially dependent on the level of family income.

Sometimes tax provisions result in reductions in taxation for families with children, and (at least in the case of Germany) benefits can also be paid at higher levels to families with children. This can be seen from Table 7.

Housing benefits are sometimes paid to low-income families, as in Germany. They are usually paid at a higher rate to the unemployed than to those in-work, but this is normally because they are based on net incomes, and these are lower for those with benefit income than for those with earnings. The difference between the columns in Table 9 only reflects differences in housing benefits.

After a certain amount of time, unemployment insurance entitlement is exhausted in Germany. An alternative benefit -- Unemployment Assistance -- is paid at a lower level than the insurance benefit. Replacement rates can be calculated in exactly the same way as above. Hence, in Germany a single person who previously earned DM 53 512 would receive DM 17 510 per year; a married person DM 19 700 and a married person with two children DM 22 217. The gross replacement rates, analogous to the first row in the Table above, would be 33, 37 and 42 per cent respectively. The replacement rate for a couple is shown in Table 11. The difference between Tables 7 and 11 therefore shows how the gross value of the main benefits declines over time. Taxation, family benefits (if applicable) and housing benefits can be taken into account in exactly the same way as above. When this is done, the net income of a family which has been unemployed for 5 years can be calculated. When this is done for the German case, net incomes of DM 17 510, 19 700 and 29 300 are found for single persons, couples and couples with two children, implying replacement rates of 53, 53 and 71 per cent respectively.

Rather than Unemployment Assistance, Social Assistance might be paid to persons who have exhausted their insurance rights in other countries. Social assistance are shown in Table 11 as are all taxes, family benefits and housing benefits. However, as noted in the text, net incomes taking account of social assistance must be interpreted with care.

Annex 3

DESCRIPTION OF MICROSIMULATION MODELS

Australia   Policy Effects Model (PEM); the Australian Department of Social Security. Data from the 1989-1990 Income and Housing Costs Amenities survey. Labour force data are aged to November 1994 (*i.e.* re-weighted to reflect known changes in the structure of the population since the survey was carried out). Policy environment reflects situation as of July 1995. Because major reforms were implemented as recently as 1995, it is impossible to impute benefits correctly for some people, notably married individuals without children who are not themselves in employment but whose spouses are unemployed.

Belgium   Model of the Ministry of Finance. Data are from personal income tax returns supplemented with statistical matching of data from the Office National de l'Emploi on those with incomes below the threshold for income tax registration. Data referring to public sector employees is not included. Data and the policy environment reflect the 1993 Belgium system.

Canada   Social Policy Simulation Database and Model (SPSD/M); Statistics Canada. Data constructed by combining individual administrative data from income tax returns and unemployment claimant histories with survey data on family incomes and expenditures for the calendar year 1988. Social Assistance cannot correctly be modelled, so a typical situation has been applied. Data are aged to 1994.

Denmark   Lovmodel; Ministry of Economic Affairs. Data drawn from administrative files for 1992. The policy environment is that of 1995. Data are a stratified sub-sample of 10 932 families. The data have been converted to a snapshot picture (as typically found in household survey data) from an annual basis under various assumptions. Replacement rates for the initially employed will be underestimated because some additional benefits (in particular housing benefits) cannot be accurately measured.

Germany   Model of Dr Bernd Fritzsche; Rheinisch-Wesfälisches Institut fur Wirtschaftsforschung e.V. Data are based on the tenth wave of the Socio-Economic Panel, taken in 1992-93. Income data are adjusted to 1995 wages and benefits. Policy situation reflects that of 1996. Sample size is 5 047 households. Civil servants are excluded.

Ireland   SWITCH model; Dr Tim Callan, the Economic and Social Research Institute, Dublin. Based on the 1987 ESRI Survey of Income Distribution, Poverty and Usage of State Services. Data are aged to 1994. Definition of METR does not take into account all benefits; some minor social assistance benefits may be excluded for technical reasons. 5 663 individuals included.

Italy   ITAXMOD; Istituto di Studi per la Programmazione Economica. Based on the 1991 Bank of Italy Survey of Household Incomes and Wealth. Data are aged to 1994. Policy environment is 1994. The sample includes 24 913 individuals. Non-employed are assumed to find jobs as clerical workers in the industry sector (which gives a typical social security contribution rate).

New Zealand   Model of the Forecasting and Cost Modelling Unit; Social Policy Agency.

Norway   LOTTE tax and transfer model. Data and the policy environment are from 1993. Data is taken from full-year survey and register data, with the Norwegian Income and Wealth Survey being the primary source. Data has then been converted to give a snapshot picture of the incentives position at one point in time (as in Denmark and Sweden). Adult children living with their parents have been excluded from the potential labour force. Housing benefit is not included (this is not an important benefit in Norway).

Sweden Model of the Economics Department, Ministry of Finance. Data is taken from the Income Distribution Survey of 1993, and has been statically updated to 1996. The policy environment modelled is that of 1996. 10 000 households are included in the sample. The data source gives annualised income (as in Denmark and Norway); it has been transformed to give a snapshot picture. All social security contributions are treated as taxes. For modelling the benefit situation of those currently employed as if they were long-term unemployed (not reported in this paper) the recommended level of social assistance has been included.

United Kingdom EBOR-TAX; model of Dr Alan Duncan, Department of Economics and Related Studies, University of York. Based on 1993 Family Expenditure Survey. Sample of 8 360 households. Policy environment is that of 1995.

United States Model of Professor John Karl Scholz, Dale Knapp, and Scott Houser; Department of Economics, University of Wisconsin-Madison. Based on data from 1990 Survey of Income and Program Participation. Policy environment is that of 1990. State benefit and income taxes are modelled.

REFERENCES

ALSTOTT, A. L. (1994), 'The earned income tax credit and some fundamental institutional dilemmas of tax-transfer integration', *National Tax Journal,* volume 47, no. 3, pp. 609-619.

ALSTOTT, A. L. (1995), 'The earned income tax credit and the over-simplified case for tax-based welfare reform', *Harvard Law Review,* volume 108.

ATKINSON, A. B. and MICKLEWRIGHT, J. (1991) 'Unemployment compensation and labour market transitions: a critical review', *Journal of Economic Literature,* Vol. XXIX, no. 4, pp. 1679-1727.

AUSTRALIA (1994), *Working Nation: The White Paper on Employment and Growth,* Canberra.

BELGIUM, BUREAU FÉDÉRAL DU PLAN, (1995) 'Variantes de réduction des cotisations sociales employeurs et de modalités de financement alternatives', Planning Paper no. 75, December.

BLONDAL, S. and PEARSON, M. A. (1995), 'Unemployment and other non-employment benefits', *Oxford Review of Economic Policy,* vol. 11, no 1, pp 136-169.

BRADBURY, B. (1995), 'Added, subtracted or just different: why do the wives of unemployed men have such low employment rates?', *Australian Bulletin of Labour,* vol. 21, no. 1, pp. 25-47.

BRADBURY B., KING, M. and McHUGH J. (1995*), Why Do the Wives of Unemployed Men Have Such Low Employment Rates?,* Social Policy Research Centre, Sydney.

CALLAN, T., O'DONOGHUE, C., O'NEILL, C. (1994), *Analysis of Basic Income Schemes for Ireland,* Economic and Social Research Institute, Dublin.

CALLENDER, C., COURT, G., THOMPSON, M. and PATCH, A. (1994), *Employers and Family Credit*, Research Report no. 32, Department of Social Security, HMSO, London.

COOKE, K. (1987), 'The withdrawal from paid work of the wives of unemployed men: a review of research', *Journal of Social Policy,* vol. 16, no. 3, pp. 371-382.

CORDEN, A. and CRAIG, P. (1991), *Perceptions of Family Credit*, HMSO, London.

DAVIES, G., DILNOT, A. W., GILES, C. and WALTON, D. (1994), *Options for 1995: the Green Budget*, Institute for Fiscal Studies, London.

DAVIES, R. B., ELIAS, P. and PENN, R. (1992), 'The relationship between a husband's unemployment and his wife's participation in the labour force', *Oxford Bulletin of Economics and Statistics,* vol. 54, no. 2, pp. 145-171.

DENMARK, MINISTRY OF FINANCE (1995), 'Unemployment traps and poverty traps -- what matters for the trade-off?', Working Paper no. 5, Ministry of Finance, Copenhagen.

DICKERT, S., HOUSER, S. and SCHOLZ, J. K. (1995), 'The earned income tax credit and transfer programs: a study of labour market and program participation', pp. 1-50 in Poterba, J. (ed.), *Tax Policy and the Economy, vol. 9,* MIT Press and the National Bureau of Economic Research, Cambridge.

DILNOT, A. W. and DUNCAN, A. S. (1992), 'Lone mothers, family credit and paid work', *Fiscal Studies,* vol. 13, no. 1, pp. 1-21.

DUNCAN, A. S. and GILES, C. (1996), 'Labour supply incentives and recent family credit reforms', *Economic Journal,* vol. 106, pp. 142-155.

DUNCAN, A. S., GILES, C. and WEBB, S. J. (1994*), Social Security and Women's Independent Incomes*, Equal Opportunities Commission, Manchester.

EARDLEY, T., BRADSHAW, J., DITCH, J., GOUGH, I. and WHITEFORD, P. (1996), *Social Assistance in the OECD Countries*, HMSO, London.

EISSA, N. and LEIBMAN, J. B. (1995), 'Labour supply response to the earned income tax credit', Working Paper no. 5158, National Bureau of Economic Research.

ERGAS, Y (1990), 'Child-care policies in comparative perspective: an introductory discussion', in OECD (1990*), Lone-Parent Families: the Economic Challenge*, OECD, Paris.

ERMISCH, J (1990), 'Demographic aspects of the growing number of lone-parent families', in OECD (1990*), Lone-Parent Families: the Economic Challenge*, OECD, Paris.

EUROPEAN COMMISSION (1993), *Growth, Competitiveness and Employment,* COM(93)700, Brussels.

EUROSTAT (1995), *Demographic Statistics,* Luxembourg.

EUROSTAT (1996), *Structures of the Taxation Systems in the European Union*, Luxembourg.

FIELD, F. (1995), *Making Welfare Work,* Institute of Community Studies, London.

FRANCE, MINISTÈRE DES FINANCES (1993), *Projet de Loi de Finances pour 1993 : Evaluation des voies et moyens, Tome II,* Imprimerie Nationale, Paris.

FRY, V. and STARK, G. K. (1993), *The Take-Up of Means-Tested Benefits 1984-90*, Institute for Fiscal Studies, London.

GARMAN, A., REDMOND, G. and LONSDALE, S. (1992), *Incomes In and Out of Work, A Cohort Study of Newly Unemployed Men and Women,* Research Report no. 7, Department of Social Security, HMSO, London.

GAUTIÉ, B. GAZIER, B., SILVERA, R., ANXO, D., AUER, P. and LEFRESNE, F. (1994*), Les subventions à l'emploi: Analyse et expériences européennes*, Document Travail et Emploi, La Documentation Française, Paris.

GIANNARELLI, L. and STEUERLE, E. (1994), 'It's not what you make, it's what you keep: tax rates faced by AFDC recipients', paper presented to the Association for Public Policy Analysis and Management conference, Chicago, October.

GIANNELLI, G. and MICKLEWRIGHT, J. (1995), 'Why do women married to unemployed men have low participation rates?', *Bulletin of Economics and Statistics,* vol. 57 no. 4, pp. 471-486.

GREGG, P. and WADSWORTH, J. (1996), 'It takes two: Concentration of employment in families in OECD countries', mimeo., London School of Economics.

HAYGHE, M.V. (1990) 'Change in American families', *Monthly Labour Review*, March 1990, pp. 114-119.

HEADY, P. and SMYTH, M. (1989), *Living standards during unemployment: the results, Volume I,* HMSO, London.

HOLT, S. (1992), 'Improvement of the advance payment option of the earned income tax credit', *Tax Notes*, vol. 60, p. 1583.

HOLTZBLATT, J., McGUBBIN, J. and GILLETTE, R. (1994), 'Promoting work through the EITC', *National Tax Journal,* vol. 47, no. 3, pp. 591-607.

IRELAND, DEPARTMENT OF ENTERPRISE AND EMPLOYMENT (1996), *Growing and Sharing Our Employment: Strategy Paper on the Labour Market,* Dublin.

JACKSON, M. (1996), *Helping Ourselves: New Zealand's Green Dollar Exchanges,* Ph.D. thesis, La Trobe University, Bendigo.

JOHNSON, T. and PENCAVEL, J. (1982), 'Forecasting the effects of a negative income tax program', *Industrial and Labour Relations Review,* vol. 35, pp. 221-234.

JOHNSON, T. and PENCAVEL, J. (1984), 'Dynamic hours of work functions for husbands, wives and single females', *Econometrica*, vol. 52, pp. 363-389.

KEELEY, M. and ROBINS, P., 'The design of social experiments: a critique of the Conlisk-Watts assignment model and its application to the Seattle and Denver income maintenance experiments', *Research in Labour Economics,* vol. 3, pp. 203-233.

KELL, M. and WRIGHT, J. (1990) 'Benefits and the labour supply of women married to unemployed men', *Economic Journal,* vol. 100, pp. 119-126.

KERSTEN, A., JEHOEL, G., SMIT, L., SIEGERS, J. and VAN OORSCHOT, W. (1993), *Samen zonder werk? Niet geïndividualiseerde sociale zekerheidsuitkeringen en de arbeidsparticipatie van vrouwen*, SVR Report R 93/7, Zoetemeer: Sociale Verzerkeringsraad.

LIETAER, B. (1994), 'Community currencies: a new tool for the 21st century', *World Business Academy Perspectives,* vol. 8, no. 2, pp. 80-97.

LUI-GURR, S., MIJANOVICH, T. and CURRIE VERNON, S. (1994), *Making Work Pay Better than Welfare: An Early Look at the Self-Sufficiency Project',* Social Research and Documentation Corporation, Vancouver.

MARSH, A. and McKAY, S. (1993). *Families, Work and Benefits,* Policy Studies Institute, London.

MARTIN, J. P. (1996), 'Measures of replacement rates for the purpose of international comparisons: a note', *OECD Economic Studies,* forthcoming.

MEYER, B. D. (1995), 'Lessons from the US unemployment insurance experiments', *Journal of Economic Literature,* vol. XXXIII, pp. 91-131.

MOYLAN, S., MILLAR, J. and DAVIES, R. (1984), 'For richer, for poorer: the DHSS cohort study of unemployed men', DHSS Research Report no. 11, HMSO, London.

OECD (1991), 'Unemployment benefit rules and labour market policy', *Employment Outlook,* July, pp. 199-236.

OECD (1993*a*), 'Earnings inequality: changes in the 1980s', *Employment Outlook*, July, pp. 157-184.

OECD (1993*b*), 'Breadwinners or child-rearers: the dilemma for lone mothers', Labour Market and Social Policy Occasional Papers no. 12, OECD, Paris.

OECD (1993*c*), 'Active labour market policies: assessing macroeconomic and microeconomic effects', *Employment Outlook,* July, pp. 39-80.

OECD (1994*a*), *The OECD Jobs Study: Facts, Analysis, Strategies*, OECD, Paris.

OECD (1994*b*), *The OECD Jobs Study: Evidence and Explanations*, OECD, Paris.

OECD (1995*a*), *The OECD Jobs Study: Taxation, Employment and Unemployment*, OECD, Paris.

OECD (1995*b*), *The OECD Jobs Study: Implementing the Strategy*, OECD, Paris.

OECD (1995*c*), *The Tax/Benefit Position of Production Workers: 1995 Edition*, OECD, Paris.

OECD (1995*d), The Employment Outlook*, OECD, Paris.

OECD (1995*e), Labour Force Statistics*, OECD, Paris.

OECD (1995*g), Income Distribution in OECD Countries,* OECD, Paris.

OECD (1995*h), Purchasing Power Parities and Real Expenditures: EKS Results Volume I,* Paris.

OECD (1996*a*), *'Making work pay', Employment Outlook 1996*, pp. 25-58, OECD, Paris.

OECD (1996*b*), *Enhancing the effectiveness of active labour market policies*, OECD, Paris.

OECD (1997), *Revenue Statistics of OECD Member Countries: 1997 Edition,* OECD, Paris.

OECD (forthcoming), *The Tax/Benefit Position of Employees: 1997 Edition,* OECD, Paris.

OECD (forthcoming), *Benefits and Incentives,* OECD, Paris.

O'LEARY, C. J., SPIEGELMAN, R. G. and KLEIN, K. J. (1995), 'Do bonus offers shorten unemployment insurance spells? Results from the Washington experiment', *Journal of Policy Analysis and Management*, vol. 14, no. 2, pp. 245-269.

OLSON, L. and DAVIS, A. (1994), 'The earned income tax credit: views from the street level', Working Paper no. 94-1, Centre for Urban Affairs and Policy Research, Northwestern University.

O'NEIL, C. J. and NELSESTUEN, L. B. (1994), 'The earned income tax credit: the need for a wealth restriction for eligibility determination', *Tax Notes*, vol. 63, p. 1189.

PUNIARD, A. and HARRINGTON, C. (1993), 'Working through poverty traps: results of the survey of sole parents, pensioners and unemployed beneficiaries', *Social Security Journal,* December, pp. 1-17.

ROBINS, P. and WEST, R. (1980), 'Program participation and labour supply response', *Journal of Human Resources,* vol. 15, pp. 499-523.

ROBINS, P. and WEST, R. (1983), 'Labour supply response', pp. 91-198 in SRI International, *Final Report of the Seattle/Denver Income Maintenance Experiment,* vol. 1, *Design and Results,* United States Government Printing Office, Washington DC.

SAUNDERS, P. (1995), 'Improving work incentives in a means-tested welfare system: the 1994 Australian social security reforms', *Fiscal Studies,* vol. 16, no. 2, pp. 45-70.

SCHERER, P. (1978), 'The perverse additional worker effect in Australia', *Australian Economic Papers,* vol. 17, no 31, December, pp. 261-275.

SCHOLZ, J. K. (1990), 'The participation rate of the earned income tax credit', Working Paper, Institute for Poverty Research.

SCHOLZ, J. K. (1994), 'The earned income tax credit: participation, compliance and antipoverty effectiveness', *National Tax Journal*, vol. 47, no. 1, pp. 63-85.

SCHOLZ, J. K. (1996), 'In-work benefits in the United States: the earned income tax credit', *Economic Journal,* vol. 106, pp. 156-169.

SEIKE, A (1994), 'The employment of older people in Japan and policies to promote it', *Japan Labour Bulletin*, December 1.

SEIKE, A and SHIMADA, H (1995), 'Social security benefits and the labour supply of the elderly in Japan', in Y. Noguchi and D. Wise (eds), *Ageing in the United States and Japan*, University of Chicago Press.

SEVEN COUNTRY STUDY (1996), Unemployment Benefits and Social Assistance in Seven European Countries, HMSO, London, forthcoming.

SNESSENS, H. R. and VAN DER LINDEN, B. (1994), 'De l'optimalité des systèmes d'assurance-chômage: quelques réflexions', *Recherches Economiques de Louvain,* vol. 60, no 2.

STEUERLE, E. (1993), 'The IRS cannot control the new superterranean economy', *Tax Notes,* vol. 61, p. 1839.

UNITED KINGDOM, DEPARTMENT OF SOCIAL SECURITY (1994), *Social Security Statistics,* HMSO, London.

UNITED KINGDOM, DEPARTMENT OF SOCIAL SECURITY (1995*a*), *Tax Benefit Model Tables,* Government Statistical Service, London.

UNITED KINGDOM, DEPARTMENT OF SOCIAL SECURITY (1995*b*), *Piloting Change in Social Security: Helping People into Work,* Department of Social Security, London.

UNITED KINGDOM, OFFICE OF POPULATION CENSUSES AND SURVEYS (1995), *General Household Survey,* HMSO, London.

UNITED STATES, GENERAL ACCOUNTING OFFICE (1992), *Earned Income Tax Credit: Advance Payment Option is Not Widely Known or Understood by the Public,* United States General Accounting Office, Washington, D.C.

UNITED STATES, GENERAL ACCOUNTING OFFICE (1993), *Earned Income Tax Credit: Design and Administration Could be Improved,* United States General Accounting Office, Washington, D.C.

UNITED STATES, GENERAL ACCOUNTING OFFICE (1994), *Earned Income Credit: Data on Non-Compliance and Illegal Alien Recipients,* United States General Accounting Office, Washington, D.C.

UNITED STATES, GENERAL ACCOUNTING OFFICE (1995*a*), *Earned Income Credit: Noncompliance and Potential Eligibility Revisions,* United States General Accounting Office, Washington, D.C. UNITED STATES, GENERAL ACCOUNTING OFFICE (1995*b*), *Earned Income Credit: Targeting to the Working Poor,* United States General Accounting Office, Washington, D.C.

UNITED STATES, GENERAL ACCOUNTING OFFICE (1996), *Earned Income Credit: Profile of Tax Year 1994 Credit Recipients,* United States General Accounting Office, Washington, D.C.

UNITED STATES, HOUSE OF REPRESENTATIVES (1993), *Overview of Entitlement Programs: 1993 Green Book,* United States Government Printing Office, Washington D.C.

UNITED STATES, HOUSE OF REPRESENTATIVES (1994*a), Medicaid Source Book: Background Data and Analysis,* Washington D.C.

UNITED STATES, HOUSE OF REPRESENTATIVES (1994*b), Overview of Entitlement Programs*: 1994 Green Book, United States Government Printing Office, Washington D.C.

UNITED STATES, OFFICE OF MANAGEMENT AND BUDGET (1996), *Budget of the United States Government: Fiscal Year 1997,* Washington, D.C.

WHITEHOUSE, E. R. (1996), 'Implementing in-work benefits in different labour markets', *Economic Journal*, vol. 106, pp. 129-141.

YELOWITZ, A.S. (1995), 'The medicaid notch, labour supply and welfare participation: evidence from eligibility expansions', *Quarterly Journal of Economics*, vol. CX, no. 4, pp. 909-940.

YIN, G. and FORMAN, J. (1993), 'Redesigning the earned income tax credit programme to provide more effective assistance for the working poor', *Tax Notes*, vol. 59, no. 7, pp. 951-960.

NOTES

1   Aggregate consumption may be affected by the level of unemployment benefits. Such general equilibrium effects are not considered in this report.

2   The forthcoming OECD publication *Benefits and Incentives* will contain information for all OECD countries.

3   The Average Production Worker (APW) figures prominently in the annual OECD publication on the tax/benefit position of workers. The APW is defined as an adult full-time production worker in the manufacturing sector whose earnings are equal to the average earnings of such workers.

4   For example, in the United Kingdom, someone working 16 hours per week at £5 per hour would earn £80 gross. A lone parent would typically be entitled to benefit income of £133 per week, so there would be little incentive to work. However, with the employment-conditional benefit, Family Credit, worth in this case £68 per week, the replacement rate drops dramatically to 65 per cent. Employment-conditional benefits must be withdrawn from those with higher incomes leading to high marginal tax rates (in the United Kingdom case above, the marginal tax rate would be over 86 per cent). Assumptions are a rent of £39.25 a week and child care costs of £40 per week. Welfare foods are not taken into account. Incomes are calculated before housing costs, but after local tax (of £8.50 per week). See United Kingdom DSS (1995a) for full details of the United Kingdom tax and benefit system

5   Those over 45 also have a longer duration of benefit.

6   Although theoretically unlimited, in practice unemployment insurance in Belgium may be limited to one-and-a-half times the average duration for similar unemployed people.

7   Italy is an exception: microsimulation analysis points to much higher replacement rates than in the stylised cases. This reflects both the complexity of the Italian benefit system and in particular the Mobility allowance and Cassa Integrazione Guadagni Straordinaria and the treatment of employers' social security contributions (see Annex I).

8   Very high (over 100 per cent) replacement rates are often the result of special provisions in the benefit system. For example, in Norway the benefit level is based on income in the previous year or the average of the income over the past 3 years. A decline in earnings can leave the benefit based on the latter rule appearing to be relatively high. Furthermore, older workers are entitled to a minimum benefit based on a wage level which may be higher than current earnings, again resulting in high replacement rates.

9   Here defined as those in receipt of a benefit which includes a requirement to search for work.

10   This discussion is based on Snessens and Van den Linden (1994).

11   For example, in Canada these are limited to two-thirds of earnings and C$ 5 000 for children under 7 and C$ 3 000 for children aged 7 to 14 (1994 figures). In the United Kingdom, employer-provided child-care has not been taxed as a benefit-in-kind since 1990.

12   Until 1993 home-care-allowance could be combined with unemployment benefit resulting in still higher replacement rates. Until 1995 this was still the case for secondary earners since the allowance could be transferred to the working spouse.

13   For example, Corden and Craig (1991) report that *no-one* they interviewed who had taken a low-paid job in the United Kingdom had calculated how much Family Credit to which they were entitled.

14   Sometimes such suspicion is justified. Current benefit provisions in the United Kingdom mean that many of those who leave benefit for a job which they subsequently lose will find that they receive less housing benefit than before.

15   The head of the Commission of the French Assembly investigating the use of public funds to promote employment noted that the first role of the commission would be to identify all such schemes. He stated that 'if we, who are supposed to be competent, don't know [which schemes are available], how can an employer know about them? Therefore, he does not use all the schemes which are in theory available to him' (Michel Péricard, translation of remarks reported in *La Tribune Desfossés*, 22 March 1996). Few employers understand how Family Credit works in the United Kingdom (Callender *et al.*, 1995).

16   The rule pre-dates 1994, but it was possible to receive more than 90 per cent if total income was less than 80 per cent of the maximum unemployment benefit.

17   Maximum rents covered by housing benefit for new claimants will be restricted to the average for the type of accommodation and area.

18   An exception to the trend is Belgium, where benefit receipt has been extended to 18-21 year olds.

19   Means-tests can have effects outside the labour market as well. Assets can be held in such a way as to ensure that incomes are minimised, so avoiding the means-test. Furthermore, it has been argued that because rules seem unreasonable and cannot easily be enforced, non-compliance can become widespread, reflecting and contributing to reduced standards of public morality (see Field, 1995).

20   Moylan, Millar and Davies (1984), Cooke (1987) and Heady and Smyth (1989).

21   It has been a problem even in some nominally insurance-based systems. In Luxembourg, for example, unemployment benefit is withdrawn at a 50 per cent BRR if the spouse's income exceeds 2.5 times the minimum wage.

22   Individual income testing cannot in itself promote participation in part-time work by the wives of unemployed men, unless means tests are structured to permit this, as is the case in Australia.

23   This recommendation was in the context of a proposed payment to non-working caring parents. Recent announcements have moved towards tightening the conditionality of benefit receipt on work requirements (for example, for lone parents with older children).

24   APPORT is paid in respect of each month in which earnings exceed C$ 100. The benefit for a two-earner couple with two children earning C$ 14 000 is over $3 800. Housing allowances of up to C$ 1 080 and child-care expenses can be paid on top.

25   Other studies have focused only on the effect on hours worked and not on participation (General Accounting Office, 1993, Hoffman and Seidman, 1990 and Holtzblatt *et al.*, 1994).

26   For example, Howard Davies, the former director-general of the Confederation of British Industry and Deputy Governor of the Bank of England has suggested that such a policy might be necessary to prevent exploitation of the government by 'cowboy employers' (as reported in *The Independent*, 22 September 1995).

27   Unless part-time work is not declared to the authorities. Thus when means-tests are reduced, it is not possible to measure the extent to which any declared increase in part-time work reflects a genuine increase or simply increased reporting.

28   Lietaer (1994) and Jackson (1996).

29   This ignores any effects on aggregate consumption. According to the Belgian Bureau Fédéral du Plan (1995), a reduction in social benefits of 2 per cent without any countervailing reduction in taxation would lead to a reduction in employment of 0.1 per cent after five years.

MAIN SALES OUTLETS OF OECD PUBLICATIONS
PRINCIPAUX POINTS DE VENTE DES PUBLICATIONS DE L'OCDE

AUSTRALIA – AUSTRALIE
D.A. Information Services
648 Whitehorse Road, P.O.B 163
Mitcham, Victoria 3132   Tel. (03) 9210.7777
Fax: (03) 9210.7788

AUSTRIA – AUTRICHE
Gerold & Co.
Graben 31
Wien I   Tel. (0222) 533.50.14
Fax: (0222) 512.47.31.29

BELGIUM – BELGIQUE
Jean De Lannoy
Avenue du Roi, Koningslaan 202
B-1060 Bruxelles   Tel. (02) 538.51.69/538.08.41
Fax: (02) 538.08.41

CANADA
Renouf Publishing Company Ltd.
5369 Canotek Road
Unit 1
Ottawa, Ont. K1J 9J3   Tel. (613) 745.2665
Fax: (613) 745.7660

Stores:
71 1/2 Sparks Street
Ottawa, Ont. K1P 5R1   Tel. (613) 238.8985
Fax: (613) 238.6041

12 Adelaide Street West
Toronto, QN M5H 1L6   Tel. (416) 363.3171
Fax: (416) 363.5963

Les Éditions La Liberté Inc.
3020 Chemin Sainte-Foy
Sainte-Foy, PQ G1X 3V6   Tel. (418) 658.3763
Fax: (418) 658.3763

Federal Publications Inc.
165 University Avenue, Suite 701
Toronto, ON M5H 3B8   Tel. (416) 860.1611
Fax: (416) 860.1608

Les Publications Fédérales
1185 Université
Montréal, QC H3B 3A7   Tel. (514) 954.1633
Fax: (514) 954.1635

CHINA – CHINE
Book Dept., China National Publications
Import and Export Corporation (CNPIEC)
16 Gongti E. Road, Chaoyang District
Beijing 100020   Tel. (10) 6506-6688 Ext. 8402
(10) 6506-3101

CHINESE TAIPEI – TAIPEI CHINOIS
Good Faith Worldwide Int'l. Co. Ltd.
9th Floor, No. 118, Sec. 2
Chung Hsiao E. Road
Taipei   Tel. (02) 391.7396/391.7397
Fax: (02) 394.9176

**CZECH REPUBLIC –
RÉPUBLIQUE TCHÈQUE**
National Information Centre
NIS – prodejna
Konviktská 5
Praha 1 – 113 57   Tel. (02) 24.23.09.07
Fax: (02) 24.22.94.33
E-mail: nkposp@dec.niz.cz
Internet: http://www.nis.cz

DENMARK – DANEMARK
Munksgaard Book and Subscription Service
35, Nørre Søgade, P.O. Box 2148
DK-1016 København K   Tel. (33) 12.85.70
Fax: (33) 12.93.87

J. H. Schultz Information A/S,
Herstedvang 12,
DK – 2620 Albertslung   Tel. 43 63 23 00
Fax: 43 63 19 69
Internet: s-info@inet.uni-c.dk

EGYPT – ÉGYPTE
The Middle East Observer
41 Sherif Street
Cairo   Tel. (2) 392.6919
Fax: (2) 360.6804

FINLAND – FINLANDE
Akateeminen Kirjakauppa
Keskuskatu 1, P.O. Box 128
00100 Helsinki

Subscription Services/Agence d'abonnements :
P.O. Box 23
00100 Helsinki   Tel. (358) 9.121.4403
Fax: (358) 9.121.4450

*FRANCE
OECD/OCDE
Mail Orders/Commandes par correspondance :
2, rue André-Pascal
75775 Paris Cedex 16   Tel. 33 (0)1.45.24.82.00
Fax: 33 (0)1.49.10.42.76
Telex: 640048 OCDE
Internet: Compte.PUBSINQ@oecd.org

Orders via Minitel, France only/
Commandes par Minitel, France exclusivement :
36 15 OCDE

OECD Bookshop/Librairie de l'OCDE :
33, rue Octave-Feuillet
75016 Paris   Tel. 33 (0)1.45.24.81.81
33 (0)1.45.24.81.67

Dawson
B.P. 40
91121 Palaiseau Cedex   Tel. 01.89.10.47.00
Fax: 01.64.54.83.26

Documentation Française
29, quai Voltaire
75007 Paris   Tel. 01.40.15.70.00

Economica
49, rue Héricart
75015 Paris   Tel. 01.45.78.12.92
Fax: 01.45.75.05.67

Gibert Jeune (Droit-Économie)
6, place Saint-Michel
75006 Paris   Tel. 01.43.25.91.19

Librairie du Commerce International
10, avenue d'Iéna
75016 Paris   Tel. 01.40.73.34.60

Librairie Dunod
Université Paris-Dauphine
Place du Maréchal-de-Lattre-de-Tassigny
75016 Paris   Tel. 01.44.05.40.13

Librairie Lavoisier
11, rue Lavoisier
75008 Paris   Tel. 01.42.65.39.95

Librairie des Sciences Politiques
30, rue Saint-Guillaume
75007 Paris   Tel. 01.45.48.36.02

P.U.F.
49, boulevard Saint-Michel
75005 Paris   Tel. 01.43.25.83.40

Librairie de l'Université
12a, rue Nazareth
13100 Aix-en-Provence   Tel. 04.42.26.18.08

Documentation Française
165, rue Garibaldi
69003 Lyon   Tel. 04.78.63.32.23

Librairie Decitre
29, place Bellecour
69002 Lyon   Tel. 04.72.40.54.54

Librairie Sauramps
Le Triangle
34967 Montpellier Cedex 2   Tel. 04.67.58.85.15
Fax: 04.67.58.27.36

A la Sorbonne Actual
23, rue de l'Hôtel-des-Postes
06000 Nice   Tel. 04.93.13.77.75
Fax: 04.93.80.75.69

GERMANY – ALLEMAGNE
OECD Bonn Centre
August-Bebel-Allee 6
D-53175 Bonn   Tel. (0228) 959.120
Fax: (0228) 959.12.17

GREECE – GRÈCE
Librairie Kauffmann
Stadiou 28
10564 Athens   Tel. (01) 32.55.321
Fax: (01) 32.30.320

HONG-KONG
Swindon Book Co. Ltd.
Astoria Bldg. 3F
34 Ashley Road, Tsimshatsui
Kowloon, Hong Kong   Tel. 2376.2062
Fax: 2376.0685

HUNGARY – HONGRIE
Euro Info Service
Margitsziget, Európa Ház
1138 Budapest   Tel. (1) 111.60.61
Fax: (1) 302.50.35
E-mail: euroinfo@mail.matav.hu
Internet: http://www.euroinfo.hu//index.html

ICELAND – ISLANDE
Mál og Menning
Laugavegi 18, Pósthólf 392
121 Reykjavik   Tel. (1) 552.4240
Fax: (1) 562.3523

INDIA – INDE
Oxford Book and Stationery Co.
Scindia House
New Delhi 110001   Tel. (11) 331.5896/5308
Fax: (11) 332.2639
E-mail: oxford.publ@axcess.net.in

17 Park Street
Calcutta 700016   Tel. 240832

INDONESIA – INDONÉSIE
Pdii-Lipi
P.O. Box 4298
Jakarta 12042   Tel. (21) 573.34.67
Fax: (21) 573.34.67

IRELAND – IRLANDE
Government Supplies Agency
Publications Section
4/5 Harcourt Road
Dublin 2   Tel. 661.31.11
Fax: 475.27.60

ISRAEL – ISRAËL
Praedicta
5 Shatner Street
P.O. Box 34030
Jerusalem 91430   Tel. (2) 652.84.90/1/2
Fax: (2) 652.84.93

R.O.Y. International
P.O. Box 13056
Tel Aviv 61130   Tel. (3) 546 1423
Fax: (3) 546 1442
E-mail: royil@netvision.net.il

Palestinian Authority/Middle East:
INDEX Information Services
P.O.B. 19502
Jerusalem   Tel. (2) 627.16.34
Fax: (2) 627.12.19

ITALY – ITALIE
Libreria Commissionaria Sansoni
Via Duca di Calabria, 1/1
50125 Firenze   Tel. (055) 64.54.15
Fax: (055) 64.12.57
E-mail: licosa@ftbcc.it

Via Bartolini 29
20155 Milano   Tel. (02) 36.50.83

Editrice e Libreria Herder
Piazza Montecitorio 120
00186 Roma   Tel. 679.46.28
Fax: 678.47.51

Libreria Hoepli
Via Hoepli 5
20121 Milano   Tel. (02) 86.54.46
Fax: (02) 805.28.86

Libreria Scientifica
Dott. Lucio de Biasio 'Aeiou'
Via Coronelli, 6
20146 Milano   Tel. (02) 48.95.45.52
                                Fax: (02) 48.95.45.48

JAPAN – JAPON
OECD Tokyo Centre
Landic Akasaka Building
2-3-4 Akasaka, Minato-ku
Tokyo 107   Tel. (81.3) 3586.2016
                                Fax: (81.3) 3584.7929

KOREA – CORÉE
Kyobo Book Centre Co. Ltd.
P.O. Box 1658, Kwang Hwa Moon
Seoul   Tel. 730.78.91
                                Fax: 735.00.30

MALAYSIA – MALAISIE
University of Malaya Bookshop
University of Malaya
P.O. Box 1127, Jalan Pantai Baru
59700 Kuala Lumpur
Malaysia   Tel. 756.5000/756.5425
                                Fax: 756.3246

MEXICO – MEXIQUE
OECD Mexico Centre
Edificio INFOTEC
Av. San Fernando no. 37
Col. Toriello Guerra
Tlalpan C.P. 14050
Mexico D.F.   Tel. (525) 528.10.38
                                Fax: (525) 606.13.07
E-mail: ocde@rtn.net.mx

NETHERLANDS – PAYS-BAS
SDU Uitgeverij Plantijnstraat
Externe Fondsen
Postbus 20014
2500 EA's-Gravenhage   Tel. (070) 37.89.880
Voor bestellingen: Fax: (070) 34.75.778

Subscription Agency/   Agence d'abonnements :
SWETS & ZEITLINGER BV
Heereweg 347B
P.O. Box 830
2160 SZ Lisse   Tel. 252.435.111
                                Fax: 252.415.888

NEW ZEALAND – NOUVELLE-ZÉLANDE
GPLegislation Services
P.O. Box 12418
Thorndon, Wellington   Tel. (04) 496.5655
                                Fax: (04) 496.5698

NORWAY – NORVÈGE
NIC INFO A/S
Ostensjoveien 18
P.O. Box 6512 Etterstad
0606 Oslo   Tel. (22) 97.45.00
                                Fax: (22) 97.45.45

PAKISTAN
Mirza Book Agency
65 Shahrah Quaid-E-Azam
Lahore 54000   Tel. (42) 735.36.01
                                Fax: (42) 576.37.14

PHILIPPINE – PHILIPPINES
International Booksource Center Inc.
Rm 179/920 Cityland 10 Condo Tower 2
HV dela Costa Ext cor Valero St.
Makati Metro Manila   Tel. (632) 817 9676
                                Fax: (632) 817 1741

POLAND – POLOGNE
Ars Polona
00-950 Warszawa
Krakowskie Prezdmiescie 7   Tel. (22) 264760
                                Fax: (22) 265334

PORTUGAL
Livraria Portugal
Rua do Carmo 70-74
Apart. 2681
1200 Lisboa   Tel. (01) 347.49.82/5
                                Fax: (01) 347.02.64

SINGAPORE – SINGAPOUR
Ashgate Publishing
Asia Pacific Pte. Ltd
Golden Wheel Building, 04-03
41, Kallang Pudding Road
Singapore 349316   Tel. 741.5166
                                Fax: 742.9356

SPAIN – ESPAGNE
Mundi-Prensa Libros S.A.
Castelló 37, Apartado 1223
Madrid 28001   Tel. (91) 431.33.99
                                Fax: (91) 575.39.98
E-mail: mundiprensa@tsai.es
Internet: http://www.mundiprensa.es

Mundi-Prensa Barcelona
Consell de Cent No. 391
08009 – Barcelona   Tel. (93) 488.34.92
                                Fax: (93) 487.76.59

Libreria de la Generalitat
Palau Moja
Rambla dels Estudis, 118
08002 – Barcelona
              (Suscripciones) Tel. (93) 318.80.12
              (Publicaciones) Tel. (93) 302.67.23
                                Fax: (93) 412.18.54

SRI LANKA
Centre for Policy Research
c/o Colombo Agencies Ltd.
No. 300-304, Galle Road
Colombo 3   Tel. (1) 574240, 573551-2
                                Fax: (1) 575394, 510711

SWEDEN – SUÈDE
CE Fritzes AB
S–106 47 Stockholm   Tel. (08) 690.90.90
                                Fax: (08) 20.50.21

For electronic publications only/
Publications électroniques seulement
STATISTICS SWEDEN
Informationsservice
S-115 81 Stockholm   Tel. 8 783 5066
                                Fax: 8 783 4045

Subscription Agency/Agence d'abonnements :
Wennergren-Williams Info AB
P.O. Box 1305
171 25 Solna   Tel. (08) 705.97.50
                                Fax: (08) 27.00.71

Liber distribution
International organizations
Fagerstagatan 21
S-163 52 Spanga

SWITZERLAND – SUISSE
Maditec S.A. (Books and Periodicals/Livres
et périodiques)
Chemin des Palettes 4
Case postale 266
1020 Renens VD 1   Tel. (021) 635.08.65
                                Fax: (021) 635.07.80

Librairie Payot S.A.
4, place Pépinet
CP 3212
1002 Lausanne   Tel. (021) 320.25.11
                                Fax: (021) 320.25.14

Librairie Unilivres
6, rue de Candolle
1205 Genève   Tel. (022) 320.26.23
                                Fax: (022) 329.73.18

Subscription Agency/Agence d'abonnements :
Dynapresse Marketing S.A.
38, avenue Vibert
1227 Carouge   Tel. (022) 308.08.70
                                Fax: (022) 308.07.99

See also – Voir aussi :
OECD Bonn Centre
August-Bebel-Allee 6
D-53175 Bonn (Germany)   Tel. (0228) 959.120
                                Fax: (0228) 959.12.17

THAILAND – THAÏLANDE
Suksit Siam Co. Ltd.
113, 115 Fuang Nakhon Rd.
Opp. Wat Rajbopith
Bangkok 10200   Tel. (662) 225.9531/2
                                Fax: (662) 222.5188

**TRINIDAD & TOBAGO, CARIBBEAN
TRINITÉ-ET-TOBAGO, CARAÏBES**
Systematics Studies Limited
9 Watts Street
Curepe
Trinidad & Tobago, W.I.   Tel. (1809) 645.3475
                                Fax: (1809) 662.5654
E-mail: tobe@trinidad.net

TUNISIA – TUNISIE
Grande Librairie Spécialisée
Fendri Ali
Avenue Haffouz Imm El-Intilaka
Bloc B 1 Sfax 3000   Tel. (216-4) 296 855
                                Fax: (216-4) 298.270

TURKEY – TURQUIE
Kültür Yayinlari Is-Türk Ltd.
Atatürk Bulvari No. 191/Kat 13
06684 Kavaklidere/Ankara
                                Tel. (312) 428.11.40 Ext. 2458
                                Fax : (312) 417.24.90
Dolmabahce Cad. No. 29
Besiktas/Istanbul   Tel. (212) 260 7188

UNITED KINGDOM – ROYAUME-UNI
The Stationery Office Ltd.
Postal orders only:
P.O. Box 276, London SW8 5DT
Gen. enquiries   Tel. (171) 873 0011
                                Fax: (171) 873 8463

The Stationery Office Ltd.
Postal orders only:
49 High Holborn, London WC1V 6HB
Branches at: Belfast, Birmingham, Bristol,
Edinburgh, Manchester

UNITED STATES – ÉTATS-UNIS
OECD Washington Center
2001 L Street N.W., Suite 650
Washington, D.C. 20036-4922 Tel. (202) 785.6323
                                Fax: (202) 785.0350
Internet: washcont@oecd.org

Subscriptions to OECD periodicals may also be
placed through main subscription agencies.

Les abonnements aux publications périodiques de
l'OCDE peuvent être souscrits auprès des
principales agences d'abonnement.

Orders and inquiries from countries where Distribu-
tors have not yet been appointed should be sent to:
OECD Publications, 2, rue André-Pascal, 75775
Paris Cedex 16, France.

Les commandes provenant de pays où l'OCDE n'a
pas encore désigné de distributeur peuvent être
adressées aux Éditions de l'OCDE, 2, rue André-
Pascal, 75775 Paris Cedex 16, France.

                                12-1996

OECD PUBLICATIONS, 2, rue André-Pascal, 75775 PARIS CEDEX 16
PRINTED IN FRANCE
(21 97 09 1 P) ISBN 92-64-15666-6 – No. 49765 1997